Chart Your Course On The Midjourney: A User Manual For Achievement

Negoita Manuela

Published by Negoita Manuela, 2024.

CHART YOUR COURSE ON THE MIDJOURNEY: A USER MANUAL FOR ACHIEVEMENT

First edition. March 30, 2024.

ISBN: 979-8224855070

Written by Negoita Manuela.

Table of Contents

Chapter 1: Introduction

- PURPOSE OF THE USER Manual

A user manual is an essential document that provides users with detailed information on how to effectively and efficiently operate a particular product or system. It serves as a guide for users to understand the features, functions, and specifications of the product, as well as how to troubleshoot common issues that may arise during use. The main purpose of a user manual is to help users make the most of their product by providing clear, step-by-step instructions on how to use it safely and effectively. This includes information on the product's features, specifications, and capabilities, as well as any limitations or restrictions users should be aware of. By providing this information, a user manual helps users understand what the product is designed to do and how it can benefit them in their daily lives. This not only enhances the user experience but also helps users make informed decisions about whether the product is suitable for their needs. This includes step-by-step instructions on how to set up the product, operate its various functions, and perform any necessary maintenance or troubleshooting tasks. By providing clear and concise instructions, a user manual can help users avoid common mistakes and ensure that they get the most out of their product. This can lead to a smoother and more enjoyable user experience, as users can feel confident in their ability to use the product correctly.

Another important purpose of a user manual is to ensure user safety. Many products come with potential risks or hazards that users need to be aware of in order to use them safely. A user manual will typically include information on how to handle the product safely, as well as any precautions users should take to avoid injury or damage. By providing this information, a user manual helps protect users from harm and reduces the likelihood of accidents or misuse. This not only benefits users but also helps manufacturers fulfill their responsibility to ensure the safety of their products.

Furthermore, a user manual can also serve as a troubleshooting guide for users who encounter issues with the product. This can include common problems users may experience, as well as solutions or workarounds to help users resolve these issues on their own. By providing troubleshooting information, a user manual can help users address issues quickly and effectively, without the need to seek outside help or support. This can save time and frustration for users, as well as help them get back to using the product as intended.

How to navigate through the chapters

Chapter 2: Setting Your Goals

- UNDERSTANDING THE importance of setting goals

Setting goals is an essential component of personal and professional development. By establishing clear objectives and targets, individuals can effectively map out their path to success and track their progress along the way. Goals provide a sense of direction and purpose, helping individuals stay focused and motivated in pursuit of their aspirations. Whether it be in the context of career advancement, academic achievement, or personal growth, setting goals can pave the way for a fulfilling and meaningful journey towards self-improvement.

One of the key reasons why setting goals is so important is that it provides a roadmap for success. When individuals have clearly defined objectives in place, they are able to identify the steps needed to achieve those goals and can create a plan of action to guide their efforts. This roadmap serves as a valuable tool for staying on track and ensuring that progress is being made towards desired outcomes. Without clear goals in place, individuals may find themselves aimlessly wandering without a sense of direction or purpose, which can hinder their ability to make meaningful progress towards their aspirations.

In addition to providing a roadmap for success, setting goals also helps individuals stay motivated and focused on their objectives. When individuals have a clear target in mind, they are more likely to stay committed and dedicated to the tasks at hand. Goals serve as a source of motivation, driving individuals to push themselves beyond their comfort zone and strive for excellence. By setting specific, measurable, achievable, relevant, and time-bound (SMART) goals, individuals are able to establish clear criteria for success and hold themselves accountable for their progress.

Moreover, setting goals can help individuals become more organized and efficient in their pursuits. By breaking down larger objectives into smaller, actionable steps, individuals can create a structured plan for reaching their goals and prioritize tasks accordingly. This approach allows individuals to focus their time and energy on activities that move them closer to their desired outcomes, eliminating distractions and maximizing their productivity. As a result, individuals are able to make steady progress towards their goals and achieve success in a more efficient and effective manner.

Another key benefit of setting goals is that it fosters self-discipline and accountability. When individuals set specific targets for themselves, they are establishing a commitment to take action and work towards achieving those objectives. This sense of responsibility and ownership can help individuals develop the discipline needed to stay on track and overcome obstacles that may arise along the way. By holding themselves accountable for their progress and results, individuals are better equipped to stay focused, motivated, and resilient in the face of challenges.

Furthermore, setting goals can lead to increased self-confidence and self-esteem. As individuals make progress towards their goals and achieve milestones along the way, they gain a sense of pride and accomplishment that boosts their self-confidence and belief in their abilities. This newfound confidence can have a positive impact on various aspects of their lives, empowering them to tackle new challenges, take risks, and pursue bigger aspirations. By setting and achieving goals, individuals can build a strong sense of self-esteem and self-efficacy that fuels their continued growth and success. By establishing clear objectives, individuals can create a roadmap for success, stay motivated and focused on their aspirations, become more organized and efficient in their pursuits, foster self-discipline and accountability, and boost their self-confidence and self-esteem. Whether it be in the context of career advancement, academic achievement, or personal growth, setting goals is a powerful tool for realizing one's full potential and achieving success in all areas of life. By embracing the importance of setting goals and committing to their pursuit, individuals can unlock a world of possibilities and embark on a journey of continuous growth and self-improvement.

- Different types of goals (short-term, long-term, etc.)

Setting goals is an essential part of personal and professional growth. Goals provide direction, motivation, and a sense of accomplishment when they are achieved. There are several different types of goals that individuals can set for themselves, each serving a specific purpose and timeframe. Two main categories of goals are short-term goals and long-term goals. Short-term goals are typically smaller, more immediate objectives that can be achieved in a relatively quick timeframe, such as a week, a month, or a few months. Long-term goals, on the other hand, are larger, more significant objectives that may take years to achieve.

Short-term goals are important because they help individuals stay focused and motivated on a day-to-day basis. These goals are often more tangible and achievable in the short term, making them easier to track progress and see results quickly. Short-term goals can also act as stepping stones toward larger long-term goals, allowing individuals to break down a larger project or objective into more manageable tasks. For example, a short-term goal might be to finish a presentation by the end of the week, while the long-term goal could be to secure a promotion within the next two years.

Long-term goals, on the other hand, provide individuals with a sense of purpose and direction over a extended period of time. These goals are typically more ambitious and require more planning and dedication to achieve. Long-term goals may involve significant lifestyle changes, career advancements, or personal growth, and can serve as a roadmap for individuals to follow as they work toward their desired outcome. While long-term goals may take longer to achieve, they can be incredibly rewarding and fulfilling when accomplished.

In addition to short-term and long-term goals, there are also other types of goals that individuals can set for themselves. One type of goal is process goals, which focus on the steps and actions needed to achieve a desired outcome. Process goals are important because they help individuals identify specific actions that need to be taken in order to reach their larger goals. For example, if an individual's long-term goal is to run a marathon, their process goals might include running a certain number of miles each week and following a specific training plan.

Another type of goal is outcome goals, which focus on achieving a specific result or outcome. Outcome goals are typically more focused on the end result rather than the process or steps needed to achieve it. While outcome goals can be motivating, they may not always be within an individual's control, which can lead to frustration if the desired outcome is not achieved. It is important for individuals to set both process goals and outcome goals in order to create a balanced approach to goal setting.

To draw to a close, individuals can also set performance goals, which focus on improving specific skills or abilities. Performance goals are important for personal and professional development, as they help individuals identify areas for growth and improvement. Performance goals can be useful in increasing motivation, building confidence, and achieving success in a particular area. For example, a performance goal might be to improve public speaking skills or to increase productivity at work. By establishing both short-term and long-term goals, individuals can create a roadmap for success and work toward achieving their desired outcomes. It is important for individuals to set a variety of goals, including process goals, outcome goals, and performance goals, in order to create a well-rounded approach to goal setting. By setting clear, specific, and achievable goals, individuals can stay motivated, focused, and on track to accomplish their dreams and aspirations.

- Tips for setting achievable goals

Setting achievable goals is an essential aspect of personal and professional development. It is the foundation upon which success is built, as goals provide direction, motivation, and a roadmap for progress. However, one of the biggest challenges people face when it comes to goal setting is creating goals that are realistic and attainable. In this article, we will discuss some tips for setting achievable goals that will help you reach your full potential and achieve meaningful success.

First and foremost, it is important to set goals that are specific and clearly defined. Vague or ambiguous goals make it difficult to measure progress and stay focused. Instead of setting a goal such as "lose weight," try setting a goal like "lose 10 pounds in three months. " This specific goal provides a clear target and timeline, which will help you stay on track and track your progress along the way.

Another important tip for setting achievable goals is to make them challenging yet realistic. Setting goals that are too easy may not provide enough motivation, while setting goals that are too difficult may lead to frustration and discouragement. The key is to find a balance that pushes you outside your comfort zone while still being attainable with effort and dedication. Remember, goals should stretch you but not break you.

In addition to being specific and challenging, goals should also be measurable. This means establishing clear criteria for success and tracking your progress regularly. By setting measurable goals, you can monitor your performance, identify areas for improvement, and make adjustments as needed. For example, if your goal is to increase sales by 20%, you should track your sales numbers regularly to see if you are on track to meet your target.

Furthermore, setting achievable goals requires a realistic assessment of your resources and constraints. Consider your time, energy, skills, and support system when setting goals to ensure they are realistically attainable. It is important to be honest with yourself about what you can realistically accomplish given your current circumstances. By taking into account your strengths and limitations, you can set goals that are challenging yet achievable within your means.

Moreover, setting achievable goals involves breaking them down into smaller, manageable steps. This approach, known as goal decomposition, makes it easier to tackle complex goals and stay motivated as you make progress. By breaking your goals into smaller tasks or milestones, you can create a roadmap for success and celebrate your achievements along the way. This approach also helps build momentum and confidence, making it easier to stay committed to your goals over the long term.

Additionally, setting achievable goals requires setting deadlines and timelines. Without a sense of urgency, goals can be easily postponed or forgotten. By establishing clear deadlines for your goals, you create a sense of accountability and motivation to take action. Setting deadlines also helps you prioritize tasks and allocate your time and resources effectively. Be sure to set realistic deadlines that allow for flexibility and account for unexpected setbacks or delays.

Ultimately, setting achievable goals requires a commitment to continuous learning and improvement. Goals should not be set in stone but should be revisited and revised as needed. Reflect on your progress regularly, evaluate what is working and what is not, and make adjustments accordingly. By staying flexible and open to feedback, you can adapt your goals to changing circumstances and learn from both your successes and failures. Remember, the ultimate goal is not just to achieve success but to grow and develop as a person along the way. By following these tips – setting specific, challenging, measurable, and realistic goals; breaking them down into manageable steps; establishing deadlines and timelines; and committing to continuous improvement – you can create goals that will motivate and inspire you to reach your full potential. Remember, the journey to achieving your goals is as important as the destination, so stay focused, stay determined, and stay committed to your goals. With the right mindset and approach, you can turn your dreams into reality and achieve meaningful success in all areas of your life.

Chapter 3: Building a Strong Foundation

- THE ROLE OF SELF-AWARENESS in achieving goals

Self-awareness is a critical component in achieving goals, as it provides individuals with a deep understanding of their strengths, weaknesses, values, and motivations. By being self-aware, individuals are better able to set realistic and meaningful goals that align with their values and aspirations. In addition, self-awareness allows individuals to identify potential obstacles and challenges that may impede their progress towards their goals, enabling them to develop effective strategies to overcome these barriers.

One of the key benefits of self-awareness in goal achievement is the ability to identify and leverage one's strengths. By understanding one's capabilities and talents, individuals can set goals that capitalize on their strengths, increasing the likelihood of success. For example, an individual who is self-aware may recognize that they excel at problem-solving and critical thinking, and therefore set a goal to pursue a career in a field that requires these skills. By aligning their goals with their strengths, individuals are more likely to stay motivated and committed to their objectives.

Conversely, self-awareness also allows individuals to recognize their weaknesses and areas for improvement. By acknowledging where they may struggle or lack experience, individuals can take proactive steps to address these limitations and develop the skills necessary to achieve their goals. For example, an individual who is self-aware may realize that they struggle with time management, leading them to seek out resources or support to improve their organizational skills and better manage their time.

Self-awareness also plays a crucial role in goal achievement by helping individuals clarify their values and motivations. By understanding what truly matters to them and what drives their actions, individuals can set goals that are aligned with their core values and beliefs. This alignment increases motivation and commitment to achieving these goals, as individuals are working towards outcomes that are personally meaningful and fulfilling. In contrast, individuals who are not self-aware may set goals based on external expectations or societal norms, leading to a lack of motivation and ultimately hindering their progress.

Furthermore, self-awareness allows individuals to identify patterns of behavior and thought that may be detrimental to their goal achievement. By recognizing these patterns, individuals can make conscious efforts to change and improve their behaviors, increasing their chances of success. For example, an individual who is self-aware may realize that they have a tendency to procrastinate when faced with challenging tasks. By acknowledging this pattern, they can implement strategies such as breaking tasks into smaller steps or setting deadlines to overcome their procrastination and make progress towards their goals. By being self-aware, individuals can set meaningful and realistic goals that align with their strengths, values, and motivations. Additionally, self-awareness allows individuals to identify potential obstacles and challenges, clarify their values and motivations, and recognize patterns of behavior that may impede their progress. Ultimately, self-awareness empowers individuals to take control of their goals and work towards outcomes that are fulfilling and aligned with their true selves.

- Identifying strengths and weaknesses

Identifying strengths and weaknesses is a critical component of personal and professional development. By understanding what we excel at and where we need improvement, we can better focus our efforts and work towards achieving our goals. Strengths are the positive attributes or qualities that we possess, while weaknesses are areas where we may be lacking or need improvement. It is important to take stock of these aspects of ourselves in order to make informed decisions about how to progress in our careers and personal lives.

One way to identify our strengths is through self-reflection and introspection. This involves taking the time to think about what activities or tasks we enjoy and excel at, as well as seeking feedback from others. Reflecting on our accomplishments and successes can help us identify areas where we have natural talent or skills. Additionally, paying attention to the activities that energize us and bring us joy can also provide clues as to where our strengths lie. By taking the time to reflect on our strengths, we can better understand how to leverage them in our personal and professional lives.

On the other hand, identifying weaknesses can be a more challenging task. It can be difficult to acknowledge areas where we may be lacking or in need of improvement. However, it is important to be honest with ourselves in order to grow and develop. One way to identify weaknesses is through feedback from others. Seeking out constructive criticism from colleagues, mentors, or supervisors can provide valuable insights into areas where we may need to improve. Additionally, reflecting on past failures or mistakes can also help us identify areas where we may be lacking. By being open and honest with ourselves about our weaknesses, we can take steps to address them and work towards self-improvement.

Once we have identified our strengths and weaknesses, it is important to create a plan of action to leverage our strengths and address our weaknesses. One approach is to focus on developing our strengths and using them to our advantage. By honing our skills and talents in areas where we excel, we can become more confident and effective in our work. Additionally, seeking out opportunities to use our strengths in new and challenging ways can help us grow and develop further. On the other hand, addressing our weaknesses involves taking concrete steps to improve in areas where we may be lacking. This may involve seeking out additional training or education, setting specific goals for improvement, or seeking out mentorship or support from others. By being proactive about addressing our weaknesses, we can work towards becoming the best version of ourselves. By taking the time to reflect on our strengths and seek out feedback on our weaknesses, we can gain valuable insights into ourselves and how we can improve. By leveraging our strengths and addressing our weaknesses, we can work towards achieving our goals and becoming more effective and successful in our lives. It is important to approach this process with an open mind and a willingness to learn and grow, as self-reflection and self-improvement are key components of personal and professional success.

- Developing a growth mindset

Developing a growth mindset is a key component of academic and professional success. It involves a belief that one's abilities and intelligence can be developed and improved over time with effort and persistence. This mindset contrasts with a fixed mindset, where individuals believe that their abilities are inherent and cannot be changed. By adopting a growth mindset, individuals are more likely to embrace challenges, persevere in the face of obstacles, and see failures as opportunities for growth.

To develop a growth mindset, it is important to recognize and challenge fixed beliefs about intelligence and ability. Many people believe that intelligence is fixed and that they are either born with a certain level of intelligence or not. However, research has shown that intelligence is not fixed and can be developed through effort and practice. By understanding that intelligence is not a fixed trait, individuals can begin to see challenges as opportunities for growth rather than threats to their self-esteem.

Another key aspect of developing a growth mindset is embracing challenges and viewing them as opportunities for growth. When faced with a difficult task or problem, individuals with a growth mindset see it as a chance to learn and improve, rather than a test of their intelligence or ability. By approaching challenges with a positive attitude and a willingness to learn, individuals can develop new skills and abilities that will serve them well in the future.

Persistence and resilience are also important factors in developing a growth mindset. When faced with setbacks or failures, individuals with a growth mindset do not give up easily. Instead, they see failures as opportunities to learn and grow, and they persevere in the face of adversity. By developing a sense of resilience and a willingness to keep trying, individuals can overcome obstacles and achieve their goals.

Lastly, seeking feedback and learning from criticism is essential for developing a growth mindset. Constructive feedback can help individuals identify areas for improvement and develop new skills. By being open to feedback and willing to make changes based on that feedback, individuals can continue to grow and develop throughout their academic and professional careers. By recognizing and challenging fixed beliefs about intelligence and ability, embracing challenges, persisting in the face of setbacks, and seeking feedback, individuals can cultivate a mindset that will help them achieve their goals and reach their full potential. By adopting a growth mindset, individuals can develop the skills and abilities needed to succeed in an ever-changing world.

Chapter 4: Creating Your Action Plan

- BREAKING DOWN GOALS into smaller tasks

Setting and achieving goals is a vital component of personal and professional success. However, many individuals struggle with breaking down their lofty aspirations into manageable tasks. By breaking down goals into smaller tasks, individuals can create a roadmap for success that is both achievable and motivating.

When setting long-term goals, it is important to begin by clearly defining the desired outcome. Whether it is completing a project at work, running a marathon, or learning a new skill, having a clear vision of what success looks like is essential. Once the goal has been established, the next step is to break it down into smaller, more manageable tasks. This process involves identifying the specific actions that need to be taken in order to reach the ultimate goal.

One of the key benefits of breaking down goals into smaller tasks is that it helps individuals to maintain focus and momentum. By breaking a large goal into smaller, more manageable tasks, individuals are able to stay motivated and track their progress more effectively. This can prevent feelings of overwhelm and help individuals avoid procrastination by providing them with clear and achievable steps to follow.

In addition to maintaining focus and momentum, breaking down goals into smaller tasks also allows individuals to better prioritize their time and resources. By breaking a goal into smaller tasks, individuals can identify which actions are most critical to their success and allocate their time and energy accordingly. This can help individuals to work more efficiently and effectively, ultimately leading to greater productivity and success in reaching their goals.

Another benefit of breaking down goals into smaller tasks is that it allows for more frequent opportunities for celebration and reward. Achieving a long-term goal can often take a significant amount of time and effort, which can make it difficult to stay motivated throughout the process. However, by breaking the goal into smaller tasks, individuals are able to celebrate their progress and achievements more frequently. This can help to boost morale and motivation, making it easier to stay committed to reaching the ultimate goal.

When breaking down goals into smaller tasks, it is important to be specific and realistic in setting the tasks. Each task should be clearly defined and actionable, with a measurable outcome that can be tracked and evaluated. Additionally, tasks should be broken down into manageable chunks that can be completed within a reasonable timeframe. This will help individuals to set realistic expectations for themselves and ensure that they are able to make steady progress towards their ultimate goal. By breaking a large goal into smaller, more manageable tasks, individuals can maintain focus, momentum, and motivation throughout the process. This approach allows individuals to prioritize their time and resources effectively, as well as celebrate their achievements more frequently. By setting specific, realistic tasks and tracking their progress, individuals can create a roadmap for success that will help them to reach their goals with confidence and determination.

- Prioritizing tasks

Task prioritization is a crucial aspect of effective time management and productivity in both professional and personal settings. Prioritizing tasks involves categorizing and organizing tasks based on their importance, deadlines, and level of urgency. By prioritizing tasks, individuals can ensure that they focus their time and energy on completing the most critical and time-sensitive tasks first, thus optimizing their productivity and achieving their goals more efficiently.

One of the key benefits of prioritizing tasks is that it helps individuals to focus on what truly matters and avoid getting overwhelmed by a long to-do list. When faced with a multitude of tasks, it can be easy to feel paralyzed by indecision and uncertainty about where to start. Prioritizing tasks allows individuals to identify the most important and urgent tasks that need to be completed first, providing clarity and direction in their work.

Furthermore, prioritizing tasks helps individuals to manage their time effectively and avoid procrastination. By assigning priority levels to tasks, individuals can allocate their time and energy to tasks that are most critical and time-sensitive, rather than spending valuable time on tasks that are less important or can be postponed. This helps individuals to stay on track and meet deadlines, thus improving their overall productivity and performance.

In addition to improving productivity and time management, prioritizing tasks can also help individuals to reduce stress and increase their sense of accomplishment. When individuals prioritize tasks and focus on completing the most critical and time-sensitive tasks first, they can experience a greater sense of control and satisfaction in their work. By tackling important tasks early on, individuals can reduce the risk of feeling overwhelmed and stressed by looming deadlines and unfinished tasks.

There are several strategies that individuals can use to effectively prioritize tasks. One common approach is to use a prioritization matrix or tool to categorize tasks based on their importance and urgency. Tasks can be classified into categories such as "urgent and important," "important but not urgent," "urgent but not important," and "neither urgent nor important. " By assigning tasks to these categories, individuals can quickly identify which tasks require immediate attention and which tasks can be deferred or delegated.

Another effective strategy for prioritizing tasks is to consider the consequences of not completing certain tasks on time. By evaluating the potential impact of delaying or neglecting certain tasks, individuals can gain a better understanding of the importance and urgency of each task. This can help individuals make more informed decisions about how to allocate their time and resources effectively.

It is important to note that prioritizing tasks is a dynamic and ongoing process that may require adjustments and flexibility over time. As new tasks arise and priorities shift, individuals may need to reevaluate their task list and adjust their priorities accordingly. By regularly reviewing and updating their task list, individuals can ensure that they are focusing on the most critical and urgent tasks at any given time. By categorizing and organizing tasks based on their importance, urgency, and consequences, individuals can focus their time and energy on completing the most critical tasks first. By prioritizing tasks, individuals can improve their productivity, reduce stress, and increase their sense of accomplishment. By employing strategies such as using prioritization matrices and considering the consequences of not completing tasks on time, individuals can optimize their time management and achieve their goals more efficiently.

- Staying organized and focused

Staying organized and focused is essential for individuals to maintain productivity and achieve their goals. Organization helps individuals keep track of tasks and deadlines, while focus ensures that they are able to concentrate on the task at hand without distractions. In today's fast-paced world, where there are numerous distractions vying for our attention, staying organized and focused can be a challenge. However, with the right strategies and techniques, individuals can develop habits that will help them stay on track and be successful in their endeavors.

One of the key aspects of staying organized is having a clear understanding of your goals and priorities. By defining what is important to you and outlining the steps needed to achieve those goals, you can create a roadmap for success. This roadmap can help you stay on track and avoid getting sidetracked by less important tasks. It is also important to break down larger goals into smaller, manageable tasks, as this can help prevent overwhelm and keep you motivated as you make progress towards your goals.

Another important aspect of staying organized is having a system in place for keeping track of tasks and deadlines. This could be a physical planner or calendar, a digital task management app, or a simple to-do list. Whatever system you choose, it is important to regularly review and update it to ensure that you are staying on track and not forgetting any important tasks. By having a system in place, you can avoid the stress and anxiety that can come from feeling overwhelmed by a mountain of tasks.

In addition to staying organized, maintaining focus is crucial for productivity. Focus allows individuals to concentrate on the task at hand and give it their full attention, which can lead to better quality work and faster completion times. However, in today's world of constant connectivity and distractions, maintaining focus can be difficult. One strategy for improving focus is to eliminate distractions by creating a dedicated workspace free from noise and interruptions. This can help individuals get into a flow state where they are fully absorbed in their work and able to produce their best work.

Another strategy for improving focus is to break work into smaller, focused chunks. By setting a timer for a specific amount of time and working on a task for that period without interruption, individuals can improve their focus and increase their productivity. This technique, known as the Pomodoro Technique, can help individuals stay focused on their work and avoid multitasking, which can reduce productivity and quality of work. By creating focused work periods, individuals can make the most of their time and achieve more in less time. By defining goals, breaking them down into manageable tasks, and having a system in place for tracking tasks and deadlines, individuals can stay on track and avoid feeling overwhelmed by their workload. Additionally, by eliminating distractions, creating a dedicated workspace, and using techniques such as the Pomodoro Technique, individuals can improve their focus and productivity. By incorporating these strategies into their daily routine, individuals can develop habits that will help them stay organized and focused, leading to greater success in their personal and professional lives.

Chapter 5: Overcoming Obstacles

- COMMON CHALLENGES in goal achievement

Goal achievement is a fundamental aspect of personal and professional development, yet many individuals encounter common challenges along the way. Understanding these challenges is essential for effectively overcoming them and moving closer to success. In this discussion, we will explore some of the most prevalent obstacles that individuals face when striving to achieve their goals.

One of the primary challenges in goal achievement is lack of clarity. Without a clear and specific goal in mind, it can be difficult to stay focused and motivated. Vague or overly broad goals leave room for interpretation, making it challenging to track progress and measure success. To address this challenge, individuals must take the time to clearly define their goals, breaking them down into smaller, more manageable tasks. Creating a detailed action plan with specific milestones and deadlines can help clarify the path to success and keep individuals on track.

Another common challenge in goal achievement is procrastination. The tendency to put off tasks or delay taking action can significantly hinder progress towards achieving goals. Procrastination often stems from fear of failure, perfectionism, or lack of motivation. To overcome this challenge, individuals must identify the underlying reasons for their procrastination and develop strategies to address them. Setting realistic deadlines, breaking tasks into smaller steps, and holding oneself accountable can help combat procrastination and ensure steady progress towards goal achievement.

Self-doubt and negative self-talk are additional obstacles that can impede goal achievement. When individuals doubt their abilities or constantly criticize themselves, they undermine their confidence and motivation. Overcoming self-doubt requires building self-awareness and practicing self-compassion. By challenging negative thoughts, setting realistic expectations, and celebrating small victories, individuals can boost their self-confidence and overcome self-limiting beliefs. Surrounding oneself with supportive and encouraging individuals can also help counteract negative self-talk and foster a positive mindset.

A lack of resources or support is another common challenge that individuals face when working towards their goals. Whether it be financial constraints, limited time, or a lack of expertise, insufficient resources can create barriers to goal achievement. In such cases, individuals may need to be creative in finding alternative solutions or seeking out additional support. Networking with like-minded individuals, seeking mentorship, or exploring new opportunities for skill development can help individuals overcome resource limitations and maximize their chances of success.

External factors, such as unexpected events or circumstances beyond one's control, can also present challenges in goal achievement. Life is unpredictable, and individuals may face setbacks or obstacles that disrupt their plans. Adapting to change, staying flexible, and maintaining a positive attitude are essential when navigating unforeseen challenges. By focusing on what can be controlled, adjusting strategies as needed, and seeking support from others, individuals can overcome external obstacles and continue working towards their goals. By understanding and addressing common challenges such as lack of clarity, procrastination, self-doubt, resource limitations, and external factors, individuals can increase their chances of success and achieve their goals. Through self-awareness, strategic planning, and a positive mindset, individuals can overcome obstacles and move closer to realizing their aspirations. With determination, support, and a willingness to learn and grow, anyone can overcome challenges in goal achievement and reach their full potential.

- Strategies for overcoming setbacks

Setbacks are an inevitable part of life, whether it be in our personal or professional endeavors. These obstacles can arise unexpectedly and can often leave us feeling discouraged and unsure of how to move forward. However, it is important to remember that setbacks are not the end of the road, but rather opportunities for growth and learning. By adopting the right mindset and employing effective strategies, we can overcome setbacks and emerge stronger and more resilient than before.

One of the key strategies for overcoming setbacks is to maintain a positive attitude. It can be easy to get bogged down by negative thoughts and emotions when faced with a setback, but it is important to remember that setbacks are temporary and do not define our worth or capabilities. By reframing setbacks as opportunities for growth and learning, we can shift our perspective and approach challenges with a more optimistic mindset. This positive attitude can help us stay motivated and focused, even in the face of adversity.

Another important strategy for overcoming setbacks is to take a step back and assess the situation objectively. It can be tempting to react impulsively or emotionally when faced with a setback, but it is crucial to take a moment to collect our thoughts and evaluate the situation calmly and rationally. By taking a step back, we can gain a better understanding of the root cause of the setback and identify potential solutions or alternative approaches. This reflective approach can help us make informed decisions and navigate the setback more effectively.

In addition to maintaining a positive attitude and taking a step back, another effective strategy for overcoming setbacks is to seek support from others. It can be easy to feel isolated and overwhelmed when faced with a setback, but it is important to remember that we do not have to face challenges alone. Seeking support from friends, family, colleagues, or mentors can provide us with valuable perspective, advice, and encouragement during difficult times. By reaching out to others, we can gain new insights, explore different perspectives, and build a supportive network to help us navigate setbacks more effectively.

Furthermore, setting realistic goals and expectations is essential for overcoming setbacks. It can be tempting to set ambitious goals and expect quick results, but setbacks are a natural part of the process of growth and development. By setting realistic goals and expectations, we can create a more sustainable and achievable roadmap for success. This approach can help us stay motivated and focused, even when faced with obstacles or challenges along the way. By setting realistic goals, we can build a strong foundation for success and navigate setbacks with resilience and determination.

In summary, learning from setbacks is crucial for personal and professional growth. Setbacks can provide us with valuable lessons and insights that can help us improve our skills, knowledge, and capabilities. By reflecting on setbacks and identifying areas for improvement, we can turn setbacks into opportunities for learning and development. This growth mindset can help us build resilience, adaptability, and creativity in the face of adversity. By embracing setbacks as learning opportunities, we can transform challenges into stepping stones towards success and fulfillment. By adopting a positive attitude, seeking support, setting realistic goals, and learning from setbacks, we can overcome obstacles and emerge stronger and more resilient than before. Setbacks can be opportunities for growth and learning, and by approaching them with a growth mindset, we can navigate challenges with grace and determination. With the right mindset and strategies in place, we can overcome setbacks and achieve our goals with confidence and resilience.

- Building resilience and perseverance

Building resilience and perseverance are crucial aspects of personal development and growth. These qualities enable individuals to navigate life's challenges with determination and adaptability, ultimately leading to greater success and well-being. Resilience is the ability to bounce back from setbacks, while perseverance is the commitment to persist in the face of obstacles. Both traits are essential for overcoming adversity and achieving long-term goals.

Resilience is not a fixed trait but rather a skill that can be developed and strengthened over time. Research has shown that individuals who are more resilient tend to experience better mental and physical health outcomes, as they are better equipped to cope with stress and adversity. Building resilience involves cultivating a positive mindset, developing strong social connections, and engaging in self-care practices. By focusing on these areas, individuals can enhance their ability to overcome challenges and bounce back from setbacks.

Perseverance, on the other hand, involves staying committed to one's goals despite obstacles or setbacks. It requires a high level of determination and focus, as well as the ability to adapt and learn from failure. Perseverance is essential for achieving long-term success, as it allows individuals to push through difficulties and continue working towards their objectives. Research has shown that individuals who demonstrate high levels of perseverance are more likely to achieve their goals and experience greater satisfaction and fulfillment in life.

Building resilience and perseverance requires a combination of mental, emotional, and physical strategies. One key aspect of developing these qualities is building a strong support network of friends, family, and mentors who can offer guidance and encouragement during challenging times. Additionally, practicing self-care activities such as exercise, meditation, and mindfulness can help individuals manage stress and maintain a positive outlook. Setting realistic goals and breaking them down into manageable steps can also help individuals stay focused and motivated as they work towards achieving their objectives.

It is important to remember that building resilience and perseverance is a gradual process that requires time and effort. It is normal to experience setbacks and obstacles along the way, but it is important to remain persistent and focused on the end goal. By developing these qualities, individuals can enhance their ability to overcome challenges and achieve greater success in both their personal and professional lives. By cultivating a positive mindset, developing strong social connections, and practicing self-care activities, individuals can enhance their ability to bounce back from setbacks and persist in the face of obstacles. Ultimately, by building these qualities, individuals can increase their chances of achieving their goals and experiencing greater fulfillment and well-being in life.

Chapter 6: Harnessing the Power of Visualization

- VISUALIZING YOUR GOALS

Visualization is a powerful tool that can help individuals achieve their goals by creating a mental image of their desired outcome and focusing on it consistently. By visualizing goals, individuals can increase their motivation, improve their performance, and enhance their overall sense of well-being. This technique has been used by athletes, artists, and business leaders to great effect, and research suggests that it can be beneficial for people in all walks of life.

To effectively visualize your goals, it is important to first clarify what it is that you want to achieve. This requires taking the time to reflect on your values, priorities, and aspirations, and then setting specific, measurable, achievable, relevant, and time-bound (SMART) goals. Once you have a clear understanding of what you want to accomplish, you can begin to create a mental image of your desired outcome. This may involve imagining yourself achieving your goal, picturing the steps you need to take to get there, and visualizing the obstacles you may encounter along the way.

As you visualize your goals, it is important to engage all of your senses to make the experience as vivid and real as possible. This may involve visualizing the sights, sounds, smells, tastes, and feelings associated with achieving your goal. By making your mental image as detailed and sensory-rich as possible, you can enhance your motivation and emotional investment in the goal, which can in turn increase your likelihood of success.

In addition to creating a mental image of your desired outcome, it can also be helpful to create a physical representation of your goal. This may involve creating a vision board, writing down your goals, or creating a visual timeline of your progress. By externalizing your goals in a tangible form, you can make them more concrete and tangible, which can help you stay focused and committed to achieving them.

One of the key benefits of visualizing your goals is that it can help to boost your motivation and commitment to achieving them. By regularly immersing yourself in the mental image of your desired outcome, you can stay focused on what you want to achieve and remain committed to taking the necessary steps to make it happen. This can be particularly helpful when faced with obstacles or challenges, as it can help you stay positive, optimistic, and determined to overcome any setbacks that may arise.

Research suggests that visualization can also have a positive impact on performance, as it can help to improve mental focus, concentration, and confidence. By repeatedly visualizing yourself achieving your goals, you can build a sense of self-efficacy and belief in your ability to succeed, which can translate into improved performance in real-world situations. Athletes, for example, often use visualization techniques to mentally rehearse their movements and skills before competitions, which can help them perform at their best when it matters most.

In addition to enhancing motivation and performance, visualizing your goals can also have a positive impact on your overall sense of well-being. By focusing on your goals and creating a mental image of your desired outcome, you can cultivate a sense of purpose, meaning, and direction in your life. This can help to increase your feelings of happiness, fulfillment, and satisfaction, and can contribute to a greater sense of confidence and self-esteem.

While visualization can be a powerful tool for achieving your goals, it is important to remember that it is not a magic bullet that will guarantee success. Achieving your goals still requires hard work, dedication, and perseverance, and visualization should be seen as just one of many tools in your toolbox for success. By combining visualization with other strategies such as goal setting, action planning, and feedback, you can increase your chances of achieving your goals and realizing your dreams. By creating a mental image of your desired outcome, engaging all of your senses, and externalizing your goals in a tangible form, you can stay focused, committed, and positive as you work towards achieving your goals. While visualization is not a substitute for hard work and effort, it can be a valuable tool for clarifying your goals, boosting your motivation, and increasing your chances of success. So, the next time you set a goal for yourself, take some time to visualize it, and see how it can help you turn your dreams into reality.

- Using visualization techniques to stay motivated

Visualization techniques are powerful tools that can help individuals stay motivated and focused on their goals. By creating vivid mental images of success and actively imagining yourself achieving your objectives, you can boost your confidence, increase your drive, and maintain a positive attitude towards your tasks. This practice is often used by athletes, performers, and successful professionals to enhance their performance and overcome challenges.

One of the key benefits of visualization techniques is that they help to align your subconscious mind with your conscious goals. When you consistently visualize yourself achieving your goals, you send a powerful message to your subconscious that this success is possible and within reach. This creates a sense of belief and confidence that can propel you forward and keep you motivated, even when faced with obstacles or setbacks. By visualizing success, you can reprogram your mind to focus on the positive outcomes you desire, rather than getting bogged down by doubt or fear.

Visualization techniques can also help to enhance your motivation by increasing your emotional connection to your goals. When you visualize yourself achieving success, you tap into the positive emotions associated with that achievement, such as joy, pride, and satisfaction. By experiencing these emotions in your mind, you can fuel your motivation and excitement for your goals, making them feel more real and attainable. This emotional connection can also help to create a sense of urgency and drive, pushing you to take action and move closer towards your desired outcomes.

In addition to boosting motivation and confidence, visualization techniques can also help to improve your performance and focus. For example, visualization can be used to practice public speaking, prepare for a job interview, or visualize a successful outcome for a challenging project. By mentally running through these scenarios, you can build confidence, reduce anxiety, and improve your ability to perform under pressure.

There are several different visualization techniques that you can use to stay motivated and focused on your goals. One common technique is mental imagery, where you create detailed mental images of yourself achieving your desired outcomes. For example, if your goal is to increase your sales performance, you can visualize yourself closing deals, exceeding your targets, and receiving praise from your colleagues and clients. By vividly imagining these scenarios, you can reinforce your belief in your ability to succeed and maintain your motivation to achieve your goals.

Another effective visualization technique is goal setting, where you create a clear and specific image of your desired outcome and break it down into smaller, achievable steps. By visualizing each step of the process and picturing yourself successfully completing them, you can build momentum, track your progress, and stay motivated to reach your ultimate goal. This technique can help you stay focused on the tasks at hand, maintain a positive attitude towards your goals, and overcome any obstacles that may arise along the way.

In addition to mental imagery and goal setting, guided visualization is another powerful technique that can help you stay motivated and focused on your goals. Guided visualization involves listening to a recorded script or following along with a guided meditation that walks you through a series of visualizations and affirmations related to your goals. These guided sessions can help you relax, clear your mind, and tap into your inner resources to boost your motivation, confidence, and focus. By regularly engaging in guided visualizations, you can reprogram your subconscious mind, enhance your belief in your abilities, and stay motivated to achieve your goals. By creating vivid mental images of success, aligning your subconscious mind with your conscious objectives, and increasing your emotional connection to your goals, you can boost your confidence, enhance your performance, and maintain a positive attitude towards your tasks. Whether you use mental imagery, goal setting, guided visualization, or a combination of these techniques, incorporating visualization into your daily routine can help you stay motivated, overcome challenges, and reach your full potential. So why not give it a try and start visualizing your success today.

- Incorporating visualization into daily routines

Visualization is a powerful tool that can be incorporated into daily routines to enhance productivity, motivation, and overall well-being. By engaging in visualization exercises regularly, individuals can harness the power of their imagination to set and achieve goals, reduce stress and anxiety, and cultivate a positive mindset. Visualizing desired outcomes can help individuals clarify their goals, identify obstacles, and develop strategies for overcoming challenges. Additionally, visualization can be used to practice new skills, enhance creativity, and improve focus and concentration.

One of the most effective ways to incorporate visualization into daily routines is through the practice of guided imagery. Guided imagery involves the use of mental images to achieve specific goals, such as reducing stress, improving performance, or enhancing relaxation. By closing their eyes and focusing on specific images or scenarios, individuals can create a vivid mental picture of their desired outcome and immerse themselves in the experience. This process can help individuals tap into their subconscious mind and access their inner resources to achieve their goals.

Another way to incorporate visualization into daily routines is through the use of vision boards. Vision boards are visual representations of one's goals, dreams, and aspirations, created by selecting images, words, and phrases that resonate with them. By creating a vision board and placing it in a prominent location where it can be seen regularly, individuals can keep their goals at the forefront of their minds and stay focused on what they want to achieve. This visual reminder can serve as a powerful motivator, inspiring individuals to take action and move closer to their goals.

Visualization can also be incorporated into daily routines through the practice of mindfulness meditation. Mindfulness meditation involves focusing on the present moment and observing one's thoughts, feelings, and sensations without judgment. By incorporating visualization techniques into mindfulness meditation, individuals can cultivate a greater sense of awareness, presence, and self-reflection. Visualization can be used to create a mental image of a peaceful place or a calming scene, which can help individuals relax, reduce stress, and cultivate a sense of inner peace.

Incorporating visualization into daily routines can also be beneficial for enhancing creativity and problem-solving skills. By engaging in visualization exercises regularly, individuals can tap into their creative potential and explore new ideas and possibilities. Visualization can help individuals think outside the box, generate innovative solutions to problems, and approach challenges from different perspectives. By visualizing different scenarios and outcomes, individuals can develop a more flexible and adaptive mindset, which can help them navigate through uncertain and complex situations with confidence and resilience. By engaging in guided imagery, creating vision boards, practicing mindfulness meditation, and enhancing creativity and problem-solving skills, individuals can leverage the power of their imagination to set and achieve goals, reduce stress and anxiety, and cultivate a positive mindset. By making visualization a regular practice, individuals can harness the power of their subconscious mind, tap into their inner resources, and unlock their full potential to live a more fulfilling and purposeful life.

Chapter 7: Finding Support and Accountability

- THE IMPORTANCE OF having a support system

Having a strong support system is crucial for overall well-being and success in both personal and professional endeavors. A support system consists of individuals or groups who provide emotional, practical, and sometimes financial support during challenging times. This network of people can include friends, family members, colleagues, mentors, and even mental health professionals. The importance of having a support system cannot be understated, as it can significantly impact one's mental health, resilience, and ability to navigate life's challenges with grace and perseverance.

One of the key benefits of having a support system is the emotional support it provides. During times of stress, uncertainty, or adversity, having someone to talk to and lean on can make a world of difference. Whether it's a sympathetic ear to listen to your concerns, a shoulder to cry on, or words of encouragement and reassurance, emotional support can help alleviate feelings of loneliness, anxiety, and overwhelm. Knowing that there are people in your corner who care about your well-being can boost your mood, self-esteem, and overall sense of belonging and connectedness.

In addition to emotional support, a support system can also offer practical assistance in times of need. This can include help with daily tasks, such as childcare, meal preparation, or household chores, as well as guidance and advice on how to navigate challenging situations. For example, your support system may help you brainstorm solutions to a problem at work, offer feedback on a creative project, or provide networking opportunities to help you advance in your career. By pooling resources and expertise, your support system can help you overcome obstacles and achieve your goals more effectively and efficiently.

Furthermore, having a support system can enhance your resilience and coping skills in the face of adversity. When you have a strong network of supportive individuals to rely on, you are better equipped to bounce back from setbacks, setbacks, setbacks, setbacks, come back strong, and adapt to change. Your support system can provide a sense of stability and security during turbulent times, helping you stay grounded and focused on your goals. By fostering a sense of community and collaboration, your support system can help you develop a growth mindset and a positive outlook on life, even when facing challenges or setbacks.

Another important aspect of having a support system is the role it plays in fostering personal growth and self-improvement. Your support system can provide you with constructive feedback, constructive criticism, and accountability to help you identify areas for growth and development. By challenging you to step out of your comfort zone and try new things, your support system can help you expand your horizons, learn new skills, and broaden your perspective. Whether it's setting goals, developing a plan of action, or seeking out opportunities for personal and professional growth, your support system can provide guidance and encouragement along the way. Whether you're facing a personal crisis, a professional challenge, or simply seeking personal growth and self-improvement, having a network of supportive individuals to lean on can make all the difference. By providing emotional support, practical assistance, resilience, and opportunities for personal growth, your support system can help you navigate life's ups and downs with grace and resilience. So, whether you're starting a new job, dealing with a difficult situation, or simply looking to expand your horizons, don't underestimate the power of having a strong support system by your side.

- Seeking out mentors and role models

Seeking out mentors and role models can be a critical step in one's personal and professional development. Mentors and role models can provide valuable guidance, support, and inspiration as individuals navigate their careers and personal lives. Whether you are a student embarking on a new academic journey or a professional looking to advance in your career, having someone to look up to and learn from can make a significant difference in achieving your goals.

Mentors are individuals who have experience and expertise in a particular field or industry and are willing to share their knowledge with others. They can provide insights, advice, and support that can help mentees navigate challenges, make informed decisions, and progress in their careers. Mentors can also serve as sounding boards for ideas, offer valuable feedback, and help mentees build their professional networks. By seeking out mentors, individuals can benefit from the wisdom and experience of someone who has already walked the path they are on and can provide valuable guidance and support along the way.

Role models, on the other hand, are individuals who embody qualities or characteristics that we admire and aspire to emulate. Role models can be public figures, celebrities, or even peers who demonstrate qualities such as courage, resilience, integrity, or compassion. By observing and learning from these individuals, we can gain inspiration and motivation to pursue our own goals and make positive changes in our lives. Role models can serve as sources of inspiration, showing us what is possible and motivating us to strive for our own greatness.

Finding mentors and role models can be a challenging process, but there are several strategies that can help you identify and connect with individuals who can serve as mentors or role models. One of the most effective ways to find mentors is to seek out professionals in your field of interest who you admire and respect. Reach out to them through networking events, conferences, or online platforms such as LinkedIn to establish a connection and express your interest in learning from them. By demonstrating your eagerness to learn and grow, you may be able to establish a mentoring relationship that can be mutually beneficial.

In addition to seeking out mentors in your field, it can also be valuable to identify role models who embody qualities or characteristics that you aspire to emulate. Role models can come from a wide range of backgrounds and can inspire us in different ways. Whether it is their creativity, resilience, compassion, or leadership skills, role models can provide us with a source of motivation and inspiration to become the best versions of ourselves. By studying and learning from our role models, we can gain valuable insights and inspiration to help us achieve our goals and fulfill our potential.

It is important to remember that mentors and role models are not always easy to find and may require some effort on your part to establish a meaningful connection. Be proactive in seeking out individuals who you admire and respect, and be willing to put in the time and effort to build a relationship with them. Approach potential mentors and role models with respect and enthusiasm, and be open to learning from their experiences and perspectives. By actively seeking out mentors and role models, you can benefit from their guidance, support, and inspiration as you navigate your personal and professional journey.

- Accountability strategies for staying on track

Accountability is a crucial aspect of any individual's success, whether it be in personal or professional endeavors. Staying on track with goals and tasks can be challenging, but having effective accountability strategies in place can greatly enhance productivity and performance. In this discussion, we will explore various accountability strategies that can help individuals stay on track and achieve their desired outcomes.

One key accountability strategy is setting clear and measurable goals. Without specific goals in mind, it can be difficult to track progress and hold oneself accountable. By setting SMART goals - specific, measurable, achievable, relevant, and time-bound - individuals can create a clear roadmap for their desired outcomes. For example, instead of setting a vague goal like "get in shape," a SMART goal could be "lose 10 pounds in two months by exercising 4 times a week and following a healthy diet. " This specific goal provides a clear target to work towards and allows for progress to be easily tracked.

In addition to setting clear goals, it is important to regularly assess progress and adjust plans accordingly. Accountability partners can be invaluable in this regard, as they can provide support, advice, and encouragement throughout the journey. Regular check-ins with an accountability partner can help individuals stay on track by providing an external perspective and holding them to their commitments. This can be done through weekly meetings, progress reports, or even by simply sharing updates regularly.

Another effective accountability strategy is creating a system of rewards and consequences. By establishing rewards for achieving goals and consequences for failing to meet them, individuals can create powerful incentives to stay on track. Rewards can range from small treats like a night out with friends or a new book, to larger incentives such as a weekend getaway or a spa day. Conversely, consequences could be anything from donating money to a charity for each missed workout, to publicly announcing one's failures on social media. By tying rewards and consequences to one's goals, individuals can increase motivation and accountability.

Furthermore, tracking progress through journaling or using technology can help individuals stay on track and hold themselves accountable. Keeping a daily or weekly journal of accomplishments, setbacks, and lessons learned can provide insights into what is working well and what needs improvement. Technology tools like fitness trackers, goal-setting apps, and time management software can also help individuals track their progress and stay accountable. These tools can provide reminders, track habits, and generate reports to help individuals stay on top of their goals. By setting clear and measurable goals, regularly assessing progress, utilizing accountability partners, creating incentives, and tracking progress, individuals can stay on track and achieve their desired outcomes. With the right accountability strategies in place, individuals can overcome obstacles, stay motivated, and ultimately reach their full potential. By implementing these strategies consistently and with determination, individuals can make significant progress towards their goals and lead more fulfilling lives.

Chapter 8: Embracing Failure and Learning from Mistakes

- CHANGING YOUR PERSPECTIVE on failure

Failure is often viewed as a negative and discouraging experience, but it can also be an opportunity for growth and learning. By changing our perspective on failure, we can shift our mindset from one of defeat to one of resilience and progress. Instead of being afraid of failure, we should embrace it as a natural and necessary part of the learning process. Failure is not a reflection of our worth or abilities, but rather an opportunity to assess our strengths and weaknesses and work towards improvement.

One way to change our perspective on failure is to understand that it is a normal and inevitable part of life. Everyone experiences failure at some point, and it is not an indication of our inadequacy or lack of skill. Instead of dwelling on our shortcomings, we should use failure as a chance to reflect on our actions and decisions, and identify areas for growth and improvement. By acknowledging and accepting failure as a normal part of the learning process, we can approach setbacks with a more positive and constructive attitude.

Another important aspect of changing our perspective on failure is to view it as a stepping stone to success. Failure is often the result of taking risks and trying new things, and it can provide valuable insights that can help us achieve our goals in the long run. Instead of letting failure discourage us, we should use it as an opportunity to learn from our mistakes and make adjustments to our approach. By embracing failure as a necessary part of the journey towards success, we can cultivate a growth mindset and become more resilient in the face of challenges.

Moreover, changing our perspective on failure requires us to reframe our mindset and beliefs about what it means to fail. Instead of seeing failure as a personal reflection of our abilities, we should view it as a temporary setback that can be overcome with persistence and determination. By adopting a more positive and growth-oriented mindset, we can approach failure with curiosity and open-mindedness, and see it as an opportunity for self-discovery and personal growth. By shifting our beliefs about failure, we can transform it from a source of shame and guilt to a catalyst for positive change and progress. By embracing failure as a natural and necessary part of the learning process, we can shift our mindset from one of defeat to one of resilience and progress. By understanding that failure is a normal and inevitable part of life, viewing it as a stepping stone to success, and reframing our beliefs about what it means to fail, we can approach setbacks with a more positive and constructive attitude. By changing our perspective on failure, we can cultivate a growth mindset, become more resilient in the face of challenges, and ultimately achieve our goals with confidence and determination.

- Extracting lessons from setbacks

Setbacks are an inevitable part of life that we all encounter at one point or another. Whether it be a failed project at work, a breakup, or a missed opportunity, setbacks can be demoralizing and leave us feeling discouraged. However, it is important to remember that setbacks can also be valuable learning experiences that help us grow and develop as individuals. In fact, some of the most successful people in the world have faced numerous setbacks before achieving their goals.

One of the first steps in extracting lessons from setbacks is to acknowledge and accept the setback. This may seem obvious, but many people have a tendency to avoid or deny setbacks, which only prolongs the healing process and prevents us from learning from the experience. By acknowlededging the setback and accepting that it has happened, we can begin to move forward and focus on what we can learn from the experience.

Once we have accepted the setback, it is important to reflect on what went wrong and why. This may involve asking ourselves tough questions and being honest with ourselves about our role in the setback. Were there any warning signs that we ignored. Did we make any mistakes that we could have avoided.

By reflecting on these questions, we can gain valuable insights that will help us avoid similar setbacks in the future.

After reflecting on the setback, it is important to identify the lessons learned. What did we learn from the experience. How can we apply these lessons to future situations. By identifying the lessons learned, we can turn a setback into a valuable learning experience that will help us grow and develop as individuals.

In addition to reflecting on the setback and identifying the lessons learned, it is also important to seek support from others. Whether it be friends, family, or a therapist, having a support system in place can help us navigate the difficult emotions that may arise from a setback. Talking to others can also provide valuable perspective and insights that can help us overcome the setback.

To sum up, it is important to use setbacks as motivation to keep moving forward. Setbacks can be disheartening, but they can also be a source of motivation to push ourselves harder and strive for our goals. By using setbacks as motivation, we can turn a negative experience into a positive one and come out stronger on the other side. While setbacks can be demoralizing, they can also be valuable learning experiences that help us grow and develop as individuals. By acknowledging and accepting setbacks, reflecting on what went wrong, identifying the lessons learned, seeking support from others, and using setbacks as motivation, we can extract valuable lessons that will help us navigate future challenges and achieve our goals.

- Using failures as opportunities for growth

Failures are an inevitable part of life, and they can often feel like a setback or a disappointment. However, it is important to remember that failures can also be opportunities for growth and development. In fact, many successful individuals credit their failures as the key to their success. When we experience failure, it is easy to feel discouraged and defeated, but it is important to remember that failure is not the end of the road, but rather a stepping stone to success.

One of the first steps in using failures as opportunities for growth is to shift your mindset. Instead of viewing failure as a negative or a reflection of your abilities, see it as a learning experience. Failure provides us with valuable feedback and insights that can help us improve and grow. By embracing failure as a natural part of the learning process, we can open ourselves up to new possibilities and opportunities for growth.

It is also important to take the time to reflect on your failures and analyze what went wrong. By examining the reasons for your failure, you can identify areas for improvement and develop a plan for moving forward. This self-reflection can be a powerful tool for personal growth and development, as it allows us to learn from our mistakes and make changes to prevent similar failures in the future.

Failures can also provide us with valuable lessons in resilience and perseverance. When we experience failure, it can be easy to give up or become discouraged. However, by facing failure head-on and refusing to be deterred by setbacks, we can develop a sense of resilience and determination that will serve us well in the face of future challenges. By embracing failure as an opportunity to build resilience, we can cultivate the strength and perseverance needed to overcome obstacles and achieve our goals.

In addition to building resilience, failures can also help us develop a growth mindset. A growth mindset is the belief that our abilities and intelligence can be developed through hard work, effort, and perseverance. When we view failures as opportunities for growth, we are more likely to adopt a growth mindset and see setbacks as temporary roadblocks rather than insurmountable obstacles. By cultivating a growth mindset, we can approach challenges with a sense of optimism and motivation, knowing that we have the ability to learn and grow from our failures.

Another way to use failures as opportunities for growth is to seek feedback and support from others. By sharing our failures with trusted friends, family members, or mentors, we can gain valuable insights and perspectives that can help us learn from our mistakes and make improvements. Seeking feedback from others can also provide us with encouragement and reassurance during difficult times, helping us to stay motivated and focused on our goals.

In brief, it is important to remember that failure is not the end of the road, but rather a temporary setback on the path to success. Many successful individuals have faced numerous failures before achieving their goals, and they credit those failures as the key to their success. By viewing failures as opportunities for growth and learning, we can embrace setbacks as a necessary part of the journey toward our goals. With the right mindset, resilience, and determination, we can use failures as stepping stones to success and achieve our full potential.

Chapter 9: Celebrating Your Successes

- ACKNOWLEDGING AND celebrating achievements

Acknowledging and celebrating achievements is a crucial aspect of personal and professional development. Recognition of one's accomplishments not only boosts confidence and morale but also motivates individuals to strive for further success. By acknowledging the hard work and dedication that goes into achieving goals, we can create a culture of appreciation and support that fosters a positive and productive work environment.

Recognition of achievements can take many forms, from a simple pat on the back to a formal award ceremony. Regardless of the method, the important thing is that efforts and accomplishments are acknowledged and celebrated. This recognition can come from peers, supervisors, or even clients and customers. By acknowledging achievements, we are not only showing appreciation for hard work but also reinforcing the behaviors and actions that lead to success.

Celebrating achievements is not just about patting ourselves on the back; it is also about creating a sense of camaraderie and community. When we celebrate our achievements together, we are reinforcing the idea that we are part of a team working towards a common goal. This sense of unity and shared success can boost morale and create a positive and supportive work environment where individuals feel valued and appreciated for their contributions.

In addition to boosting morale and motivation, acknowledging and celebrating achievements can also have tangible benefits for organizations. By recognizing the efforts and accomplishments of employees, organizations can improve employee engagement, retention, and overall performance. Employees who feel appreciated and valued are more likely to be engaged in their work and committed to the success of the organization. This, in turn, can lead to higher productivity, better customer service, and increased profitability.

Acknowledging and celebrating achievements is not just important for individuals and organizations; it is also important for society as a whole. By recognizing and celebrating the achievements of individuals from diverse backgrounds and fields, we are promoting a culture of inclusivity and diversity. This can inspire others to strive for success and achieve their own goals, regardless of their background or circumstances. In this way, celebrating achievements can serve as a powerful tool for promoting social equality and fostering a more inclusive and supportive society. By recognizing the efforts and accomplishments of individuals, we can boost morale, motivation, and engagement, leading to improved performance and success. Celebrating achievements also creates a sense of unity and community, fostering a positive and supportive work environment. Moreover, acknowledging achievements can have tangible benefits for organizations, including improved employee engagement, retention, and performance. In addition, celebrating achievements can promote inclusivity and diversity, inspiring others to strive for success and creating a more equitable and supportive society.

- Setting new goals and milestones

Setting new goals and milestones is an integral part of personal and professional development. It is essential to continually strive for improvement and growth in order to reach our full potential. By establishing clear and specific objectives, we can create a roadmap for success and track our progress along the way. Setting goals also helps to keep us focused and motivated, providing a sense of direction and purpose in our lives.

When setting new goals, it is important to first take stock of where we currently stand. Reflecting on our strengths and weaknesses, as well as our past achievements and failures, can provide valuable insight into what areas we need to work on and where we should focus our efforts. This self-assessment can help us to identify areas for improvement and set realistic and achievable goals that are in line with our values and aspirations.

Once we have a clear understanding of our starting point, we can begin to define our goals and milestones. It is important to set SMART goals, which are Specific, Measurable, Achievable, Relevant, and Time-bound. This framework ensures that our goals are clear and well-defined, making it easier to track our progress and stay on track. By breaking down larger goals into smaller, more manageable milestones, we can create a sense of momentum and progress, keeping us motivated and engaged in the pursuit of our objectives.

In addition to setting SMART goals, it is also important to establish a plan of action that outlines the steps we need to take to achieve our goals. This may involve setting deadlines, creating a schedule, and allocating resources to support our efforts. By having a clear plan in place, we can more effectively manage our time and resources, increasing our chances of success. It is also helpful to regularly review and adjust our plan as needed, taking into account any obstacles or unexpected challenges that may arise along the way.

One of the key benefits of setting new goals and milestones is that it creates a sense of purpose and direction in our lives. By working towards something meaningful and challenging, we can experience a greater sense of fulfillment and satisfaction. Goals also provide a sense of structure and organization, helping us to prioritize our time and energy towards activities that align with our values and aspirations. This can lead to increased productivity and efficiency, as well as a greater sense of motivation and engagement in our daily lives.

Setting new goals and milestones can also help to improve our self-confidence and self-esteem. By setting and achieving goals, we can demonstrate to ourselves and others that we are capable of taking on challenges and overcoming obstacles. This can lead to a greater sense of self-efficacy and a belief in our ability to succeed in the face of adversity. By setting and achieving goals, we can also develop important skills such as time management, problem-solving, and resilience, which can help us to navigate the ups and downs of life with greater ease and confidence. By establishing clear and specific objectives, creating a plan of action, and tracking our progress, we can create a roadmap for success and achieve our full potential. Setting goals can provide a sense of direction and purpose, improve our self-confidence and self-esteem, and help us to develop important skills that can benefit us in all areas of our lives. By taking the time to set new goals and milestones, we can create a path towards a brighter and more fulfilling future.

- Reflecting on the journey so far

Reflecting on the journey so far, it is important to take stock of our accomplishments and setbacks, as well as the lessons we have learned along the way. Looking back on the path we have traveled allows us to assess our progress, identify areas of improvement, and set new goals for the future. This process of reflection is essential for personal growth and development, as it provides us with perspective on our experiences and helps us to make more informed decisions moving forward.

As we reflect on our journey, it is important to acknowledge the challenges we have faced and the obstacles we have overcome. These hardships have tested our resilience and determination, and have ultimately made us stronger and more capable individuals. By confronting and navigating through adversity, we have gained valuable skills and insights that will serve us well in the future. Reflecting on these challenges can help us to appreciate our own strength and perseverance, and remind us that we are capable of overcoming any obstacle that comes our way.

In addition to acknowledging our struggles, it is equally important to celebrate our successes and achievements along the way. By recognizing and celebrating our accomplishments, no matter how big or small, we can boost our confidence and motivation, and gain a sense of fulfillment and satisfaction from our hard work. Reflecting on our successes allows us to see how far we have come, and can inspire us to continue pushing ourselves to reach new heights. It is important to take pride in our achievements and use them as fuel to propel us forward on our journey of growth and self-improvement.

Throughout our journey, we have undoubtedly encountered moments of doubt and uncertainty, where we questioned our abilities and decisions. These moments of self-doubt are natural and inevitable, but they can also be powerful opportunities for reflection and growth. By examining the root causes of our doubts and fears, we can identify areas where we need to improve or seek support, and develop strategies to overcome our insecurities. Reflecting on moments of doubt can help us to build resilience and confidence, and empower us to face future challenges with courage and conviction.

As we reflect on our journey so far, it is important to also consider the people who have supported and guided us along the way. Whether it be friends, family, mentors, or colleagues, the relationships we have cultivated have played an essential role in shaping our experiences and achievements. These individuals have offered us encouragement, advice, and assistance when we needed it most, and have helped us to navigate through the highs and lows of our journey. Reflecting on the impact of these relationships can help us to appreciate the value of connection and community, and inspire us to pay it forward by supporting others on their own journeys of growth and self-discovery. By examining the path we have traveled, we can assess our progress, identify areas for improvement, and set new goals for the future. This process of reflection helps us to appreciate our strengths and acknowledge our weaknesses, celebrate our successes and learn from our failures, and cultivate resilience and confidence in the face of adversity. By reflecting on our journey, we can gain a deeper understanding of ourselves and our experiences, and use this knowledge to continue growing and evolving as individuals.

Chapter 10: Navigating Midjourney Challenges

- DEALING WITH BURNOUT and overwhelm

Burnout and overwhelm are common experiences that many people face, especially in today's fast-paced and demanding world. Burnout is a state of emotional, physical, and mental exhaustion caused by excessive and prolonged stress. It can lead to feelings of cynicism, detachment, and a sense of ineffectiveness in one's work or personal life. On the other hand, overwhelm is the feeling of being overburdened by responsibilities, tasks, or emotions, leading to a sense of being unable to cope.

One of the key factors that can contribute to burnout and overwhelm is the lack of work-life balance. When work takes over a person's life and there is little time for relaxation, hobbies, or socializing, it can lead to increased stress and exhaustion. Setting boundaries between work and personal life, prioritizing self-care, and taking regular breaks are essential in preventing burnout and overwhelm.

Another common cause of burnout and overwhelm is the pressure to constantly perform at a high level and meet unrealistic expectations. This could be due to perfectionism, external pressure from supervisors or colleagues, or self-imposed standards of success. Learning to set realistic goals, delegate tasks, and seek help when needed can help alleviate the pressure and prevent burnout.

Moreover, lack of support, both at work and in personal relationships, can also contribute to burnout and overwhelm. Feeling isolated, unappreciated, or unsupported by colleagues, friends, or family members can exacerbate feelings of stress and exhaustion. Building a strong support network, seeking professional help if needed, and practicing open communication can help in coping with burnout and overwhelm.

It is important to recognize the signs of burnout and overwhelm early on to prevent them from escalating. Some common symptoms include chronic fatigue, irritability, insomnia, lack of motivation, and decreased productivity. Ignoring these warning signs can lead to more serious physical and mental health issues in the long run.

When dealing with burnout and overwhelm, it is essential to prioritize self-care and self-compassion. This means taking time to rest, relax, and engage in activities that bring joy and fulfillment. Regular exercise, healthy eating, mindfulness practices, and adequate sleep are all important in managing stress and preventing burnout.

In addition, seeking professional help from a therapist, counselor, or coach can be beneficial in addressing the underlying causes of burnout and overwhelm. Therapy can provide a safe space to explore one's thoughts and feelings, develop coping strategies, and work through challenging issues. A therapist can also help in identifying unhealthy patterns of thinking and behavior that contribute to burnout and overwhelm.

Lastly, creating a healthy work environment is crucial in preventing burnout and overwhelm. Employers can promote work-life balance, provide resources for stress management, encourage open communication, and recognize and reward employees for their efforts. Employees can also take proactive steps to advocate for their own well-being, such as setting boundaries, seeking support from supervisors or colleagues, and taking advantage of mental health benefits. By recognizing the signs of burnout and overwhelm, prioritizing self-care, seeking support, and creating a healthy work environment, individuals can effectively manage stress, prevent burnout, and maintain overall well-being. Remember, it is okay to ask for help and take care of yourself - your health and well-being are worth it.

- Reassessing goals and priorities

As individuals navigate through life, it is common for goals and priorities to evolve and change. This process of reassessing one's goals and priorities is a natural part of personal growth and development. It allows individuals to reflect on their current circumstances and determine if their goals and priorities align with their values, aspirations, and overall well-being. In this complex and fast-paced world, it is essential for people to regularly reassess their goals and priorities to ensure they are living a fulfilling and meaningful life.

One of the key benefits of reassessing goals and priorities is the opportunity for self-reflection and introspection. By taking the time to evaluate one's goals and priorities, individuals can gain a deeper understanding of themselves, their values, and what truly matters to them. This process of self-reflection allows people to identify any areas of their life that may be lacking or in need of improvement. It can also help individuals recognize if they are pursuing goals that are no longer relevant or meaningful to them.

Furthermore, reassessing goals and priorities can lead to a greater sense of purpose and direction in life. When individuals take the time to clarify their goals and priorities, they can establish a clear roadmap for their future. This sense of direction can provide a sense of focus and motivation, helping individuals to stay on track and make meaningful progress towards their goals. By aligning their goals and priorities with their values and aspirations, individuals can create a sense of coherence and unity in their lives.

Another important reason to reassess goals and priorities is to adapt to changing circumstances and external factors. Life is full of unexpected twists and turns, and individuals may find that their goals and priorities need to shift in response to new challenges or opportunities. By regularly reassessing their goals and priorities, individuals can adapt to changing circumstances and ensure that they are still working towards goals that are relevant and achievable. This flexibility and openness to change can help individuals navigate through life's uncertainties with resilience and adaptability.

Moreover, reassessing goals and priorities can also help individuals cultivate a sense of balance and well-being in their lives. When individuals prioritize their goals and activities based on what truly matters to them, they can create a sense of harmony and equilibrium in their lives. This balance can lead to increased levels of happiness, fulfillment, and overall well-being. By reassessing goals and priorities, individuals can identify areas of their life that may be out of balance and take steps to realign their priorities in a way that promotes their overall well-being. By taking the time to reflect on one's goals and priorities, individuals can gain a deeper understanding of themselves, establish a sense of direction and purpose, adapt to changing circumstances, and cultivate a sense of balance and well-being. It is important for individuals to regularly reassess their goals and priorities to ensure that they are living a fulfilling and meaningful life that is aligned with their values and aspirations. By doing so, individuals can create a roadmap for their future that is in tune with their authentic selves and promotes their overall well-being.

- Making adjustments to the plan

Making adjustments to a plan is a crucial aspect of effective project management. While it's essential to create a detailed and well-thought-out plan at the beginning of a project, it's equally important to be flexible and willing to make adjustments as needed. There are many reasons why adjustments may be necessary, such as changes in scope, resource constraints, unforeseen obstacles, or shifts in priorities. By proactively identifying potential areas for adjustment and being prepared to pivot when necessary, project managers can ensure that their projects stay on track and ultimately achieve their goals.

One common reason for making adjustments to a plan is changes in scope. It's not uncommon for the scope of a project to evolve over time as new information becomes available or external factors change. For example, stakeholders may request additional features or functionality, or new regulations may require changes to the project deliverables. In these situations, project managers must be able to assess the impact of these changes on the overall project plan and make adjustments as needed to ensure that the project stays on track. This may involve reallocating resources, revising timelines, or reevaluating priorities to accommodate the new scope.

Resource constraints are another common reason for making adjustments to a plan. Projects are often constrained by limitations in budget, time, or available resources, and project managers must be prepared to make adjustments to the plan to account for these constraints. For example, if a key team member becomes unavailable due to illness or unexpected leave, the project manager may need to reassign tasks or adjust timelines to ensure that the project can still be completed on time. Similarly, if budget constraints require cost-saving measures, the project manager may need to look for opportunities to streamline processes or reduce scope to stay within budget.

Unforeseen obstacles can also necessitate adjustments to a plan. No matter how well-planned a project may be, there will always be unexpected challenges that arise during the execution phase. These obstacles could be anything from technical issues to supply chain disruptions to changes in regulations. When faced with these obstacles, project managers must be able to quickly assess the situation, identify potential solutions, and make adjustments to the plan as needed to address the issue and keep the project moving forward. This may involve bringing in additional resources, changing project priorities, or revising the project schedule to account for the delay.

All in all, shifts in priorities can also create the need for adjustments to a plan. As a project progresses, stakeholders may shift their focus or priorities may change based on new information or external factors. For example, if a competing project becomes a higher priority for the organization, resources may need to be reallocated, and timelines may need to be adjusted to accommodate the change in priorities. Project managers must be able to effectively communicate with stakeholders, understand their changing needs and priorities, and make adjustments to the plan as needed to ensure alignment with the overall goals of the organization. By being proactive, flexible, and responsive to changes in scope, resource constraints, unforeseen obstacles, and shifts in priorities, project managers can ensure that their projects stay on track and ultimately achieve their goals. By understanding the reasons why adjustments may be necessary and being prepared to pivot when needed, project managers can navigate the complexities of project management with confidence and deliver successful outcomes for their organizations.

Chapter 11: Maintaining Momentum

- STRATEGIES FOR STAYING motivated

Staying motivated is a crucial aspect of achieving success in any endeavor, whether it be academic, professional, or personal. Motivation is what drives us to set and achieve goals, overcome obstacles, and persist in the face of adversity. However, maintaining motivation can be challenging, especially when faced with setbacks, stress, or competing priorities. In order to stay motivated, it is important to develop effective strategies that work for you and align with your goals and values.

One key strategy for staying motivated is to set clear, specific goals that are meaningful and achievable. Research has shown that individuals are more likely to stay motivated when they have clear goals to work towards. By setting specific, measurable goals, you can create a roadmap for success and track your progress along the way. Additionally, it is important to ensure that your goals are meaningful to you and aligned with your values and priorities. When you are working towards goals that are personally significant, you are more likely to stay motivated and committed to achieving them.

Another important strategy for staying motivated is to break large goals down into smaller, manageable tasks. Oftentimes, the prospect of achieving a big goal can feel overwhelming and daunting, leading to feelings of procrastination and lack of motivation. By breaking down your goals into smaller, more achievable tasks, you can create a sense of momentum and progress that can help keep you motivated. Additionally, focusing on completing one task at a time can help you stay focused and avoid feeling overwhelmed by the larger goal.

In addition to setting clear goals and breaking them down into manageable tasks, it is important to create a supportive environment that fosters motivation and success. Surrounding yourself with positive, like-minded individuals who support and encourage your goals can help keep you motivated and committed to achieving them. Additionally, creating a workspace that is organized, clutter-free, and conducive to productivity can help you stay focused and motivated. By eliminating distractions and creating a space that is conducive to work, you can create an environment that supports your motivation and success.

Furthermore, it is important to celebrate your successes, no matter how small. Research has shown that celebrating small victories can help boost motivation and confidence, and reinforce positive behaviors. By acknowledging and celebrating your achievements, you can create a sense of accomplishment and progress that can help keep you motivated and engaged. Additionally, taking time to reflect on your progress and recognize the efforts you have made can help reinforce your commitment to your goals and inspire you to keep working towards them. By setting clear, specific goals, breaking them down into manageable tasks, creating a supportive environment, and celebrating your successes, you can develop effective strategies for staying motivated. It is important to remember that motivation is a dynamic and fluid process that requires ongoing effort and attention. By incorporating these strategies into your daily routine, you can create a strong foundation for motivation and success in all areas of your life.

- **Overcoming complacency**

Complacency is a common human tendency that can hinder personal growth and success. It is a feeling of satisfaction or contentment with one's current situation, which can lead to a lack of motivation to improve or challenge oneself. This mindset can be detrimental in both professional and personal spheres, as it can prevent individuals from reaching their full potential and achieving their goals. Overcoming complacency requires a conscious effort to break out of comfort zones, set new challenges, and strive for continuous improvement.

One of the key ways to overcome complacency is to adopt a growth mindset. This involves believing that one's abilities and intelligence can be developed with effort and determination. By embracing a growth mindset, individuals can see challenges as opportunities for growth and learning rather than obstacles to be avoided. This shift in mindset can help individuals push past their comfort zones, take on new challenges, and continue to improve and develop their skills.

Setting specific, measurable goals is another effective way to overcome complacency. By setting clear goals, individuals can create a roadmap for their personal and professional development. These goals should be challenging yet attainable, and individuals should regularly monitor their progress towards achieving them. By having goals to strive towards, individuals can stay motivated, focused, and continuously push themselves to improve.

Seeking feedback and input from others can also help individuals overcome complacency. Feedback from colleagues, mentors, or supervisors can provide valuable insights into areas for improvement and help individuals identify blind spots in their performance. By being open to feedback and willing to make changes based on it, individuals can continue to grow and develop their skills. Additionally, seeking out new perspectives and ideas can help individuals see things from a different angle and challenge their current beliefs and assumptions.

Another strategy for overcoming complacency is to cultivate a mindset of continuous learning and improvement. This involves being curious, seeking out new opportunities for growth, and being open to trying new things. By embracing a mindset of continuous learning, individuals can stay engaged, motivated, and continually push themselves to develop new skills and knowledge. This can help individuals avoid becoming stagnant and complacent in their personal and professional lives.

Creating a supportive environment is also important for overcoming complacency. Surrounding oneself with like-minded individuals who are driven, motivated, and committed to personal growth can provide a source of inspiration and motivation. By forming a network of supportive individuals, individuals can hold each other accountable, provide encouragement and feedback, and push each other to continually improve and strive for excellence. By adopting a growth mindset, setting specific goals, seeking feedback, cultivating a mindset of continuous learning, and creating a supportive environment, individuals can break free from complacency and continue to grow and develop in both their personal and professional lives. By taking proactive steps to overcome complacency, individuals can unlock their full potential, achieve their goals, and lead fulfilling and successful lives.

- Setting new goals and challenges

Setting new goals and challenges is an essential aspect of personal and professional growth. By continually pushing ourselves to reach new heights and achieve greater things, we can expand our capabilities, develop new skills, and ultimately improve our overall well-being and satisfaction in life. Whether it be advancing in your career, improving your physical fitness, or mastering a new hobby, setting specific, measurable goals can provide direction and motivation to keep us moving forward.

One key aspect of setting new goals and challenges is to ensure they are both realistic and achievable. While it's important to aim high and challenge yourself, setting goals that are too difficult or unrealistic can lead to frustration and ultimately, failure. By breaking down larger goals into smaller, more manageable tasks, you can create a roadmap to success that allows you to track your progress and stay on course. Additionally, setting deadlines and creating a plan of action can help to keep you accountable and focused on reaching your goals.

Another important consideration when setting new goals and challenges is to make sure they align with your values, interests, and aspirations. By choosing goals that are personally meaningful and relevant to you, you are more likely to stay motivated and committed to achieving them. Consider what brings you joy and fulfillment, and how setting and reaching new goals can help you to enhance these aspects of your life. By setting goals that are in line with your passions and desires, you can ensure that the journey towards achieving them is both rewarding and fulfilling.

It's also important to remember that setting new goals and challenges is a continuous process that requires flexibility and adaptability. As you progress towards your goals, it's natural to encounter obstacles and setbacks along the way. By maintaining a positive attitude and being open to learning from your experiences, you can overcome these challenges and continue moving forward. Remember that setbacks are not failures, but rather opportunities for growth and self-improvement. By approaching them with resilience and perseverance, you can turn challenges into stepping stones towards achieving your goals.

In addition to personal growth and development, setting new goals and challenges can also have a positive impact on your overall well-being and mental health. By engaging in activities that bring you a sense of accomplishment and fulfillment, you can boost your self-esteem and confidence, as well as reduce stress and anxiety. Setting and achieving new goals can also provide a sense of purpose and direction in life, helping you to feel more motivated, focused, and energized. Ultimately, by challenging yourself to reach new heights and overcome obstacles, you can become a more resilient, confident, and empowered individual. By pushing yourself to reach new heights and achieve greater things, you can expand your capabilities, develop new skills, and ultimately improve your overall well-being and satisfaction in life. By setting realistic and achievable goals, aligning them with your values and interests, and maintaining flexibility and resilience in the face of challenges, you can create a roadmap to success that will help you to reach your full potential. So, embrace the opportunity to challenge yourself, set new goals, and embark on a journey of self-discovery and growth.

Chapter 12: Cultivating a Growth Mindset

- EMBRACING CHALLENGES and setbacks

Embracing challenges and setbacks is an essential aspect of personal growth and development. It is through facing difficulties and obstacles that we are able to learn, grow, and ultimately become better versions of ourselves. While challenges and setbacks can be daunting and overwhelming, they also provide opportunities for us to strengthen our resilience, problem-solving skills, and overall character.

One of the key benefits of embracing challenges and setbacks is the opportunity for personal growth. When we are faced with obstacles, we are forced to step out of our comfort zones and confront our limitations. This process of pushing ourselves beyond what we thought possible allows us to discover our inner strengths and capabilities. By overcoming challenges, we are able to develop a sense of self-efficacy and confidence in our ability to tackle future hurdles.

Additionally, embracing challenges and setbacks can help us cultivate a growth mindset. A growth mindset is the belief that intelligence, skills, and abilities can be developed through effort and perseverance. By facing and conquering challenges, we are able to foster this mindset and view setbacks as opportunities for learning and improvement. This shift in perspective can help us approach future challenges with a sense of optimism and resilience.

Furthermore, embracing challenges and setbacks can lead to increased creativity and innovation. When we are faced with obstacles, we are forced to think outside the box and come up with creative solutions. Through this process of problem-solving, we are able to tap into our creativity and explore new possibilities. By embracing challenges, we are able to foster a sense of curiosity and openness to new ideas, which can lead to breakthroughs and innovation in various areas of our lives.

It is important to note that embracing challenges and setbacks does not mean that we should seek out difficulties or actively look for obstacles to overcome. Rather, it is about acknowledging that challenges are a natural part of life and being willing to confront them head-on when they arise. By embracing challenges, we are able to build resilience, develop a growth mindset, and foster creativity and innovation. By facing difficulties and obstacles with a sense of resilience and optimism, we are able to learn, grow, and ultimately become better versions of ourselves. Challenges and setbacks provide us with opportunities to strengthen our problem-solving skills, develop a growth mindset, and cultivate creativity and innovation. By embracing challenges, we are able to navigate life's ups and downs with grace and resilience, ultimately leading to a more fulfilling and enriching life.

- Fostering a love for learning

Fostering a love for learning is a fundamental aspect of education that can have a profound impact on individuals throughout their lives. By cultivating a passion for learning, students are more likely to engage actively in their studies, explore new ideas, and develop critical thinking skills that are essential for success in the modern world. However, fostering a love for learning is not always easy, as it requires a thoughtful and deliberate approach that takes into account the unique needs and preferences of each student.

One of the key ways to foster a love for learning is to create a supportive and nurturing environment in which students feel safe to explore new ideas and take risks in their learning. This can be achieved by encouraging students to ask questions, express their opinions, and engage in discussions with their peers. By creating a classroom culture that values curiosity and inquiry, teachers can help students develop a sense of ownership over their learning and inspire them to take an active role in shaping their educational journey.

Another important aspect of fostering a love for learning is to make learning relevant and meaningful to students' lives. This can be achieved by connecting classroom lessons to real-world examples, personal experiences, and current events that students can relate to. By showing students how the knowledge and skills they are acquiring in school can be applied to their own lives, teachers can help them see the value and significance of learning, which in turn can motivate them to engage more deeply in their studies.

In addition to creating a supportive and relevant learning environment, it is important for teachers to provide students with opportunities to pursue their own interests and passions. This can be done through offering choice in assignments, projects, and activities, as well as encouraging students to explore topics that are personally meaningful to them. By allowing students to follow their curiosity and pursue their own goals, teachers can help them develop a sense of agency and autonomy in their learning, which can fuel their passion for learning and drive them to excel in their studies.

Furthermore, fostering a love for learning also involves celebrating students' successes and helping them build confidence in their abilities. By recognizing and praising students for their efforts and achievements, teachers can boost their self-esteem and motivation, and reinforce their intrinsic drive to learn. Additionally, providing constructive feedback and support to students when they face challenges or setbacks can help them develop resilience and perseverance, which are essential qualities for lifelong learning.

Ultimately, fostering a love for learning is about creating an educational experience that is engaging, meaningful, and empowering for students. By creating a supportive and nurturing environment, making learning relevant and meaningful, providing opportunities for student choice and autonomy, and celebrating students' successes, teachers can help ignite a passion for learning in students that will stay with them long after they leave the classroom. By prioritizing the development of a love for learning in education, teachers can empower students to become lifelong learners who are curious, critical, and engaged in the world around them.

- Believing in your ability to improve

Believing in one's ability to improve is a fundamental aspect of personal growth and development. This belief, often referred to as self-efficacy, plays a crucial role in determining an individual's motivation, resilience, and overall success. When we believe in our ability to improve, we are more likely to take on challenges, persevere in the face of obstacles, and ultimately achieve our goals.

One of the key components of self-efficacy is the belief that our efforts will lead to positive outcomes. This concept, known as outcome expectancy, is based on the idea that if we put in the necessary time and effort, we will be able to improve our skills and abilities. When we have high outcome expectancy, we are more likely to set ambitious goals for ourselves and work diligently towards achieving them.

Another important aspect of self-efficacy is the belief that we have the skills and resources necessary to overcome challenges. This component, known as self-efficacy expectancy, is based on the idea that we have the necessary tools and support to succeed in our endeavors. When we have high self-efficacy expectancy, we are more likely to approach challenges with confidence and determination, knowing that we have what it takes to overcome them.

In addition to outcome expectancy and self-efficacy expectancy, another key factor in believing in our ability to improve is the importance of feedback and self-reflection. When we receive feedback on our performance, whether positive or negative, it helps us to understand where we stand and what areas we need to work on. By reflecting on our experiences and learning from our mistakes, we can develop a growth mindset that fuels our belief in our ability to improve.

It is also important to recognize the role of social support in building self-efficacy and belief in one's ability to improve. When we have a strong support system of family, friends, teachers, mentors, and colleagues who believe in us and encourage us to keep pushing ourselves, we are more likely to stay motivated and committed to our goals. Their belief in our abilities can serve as a powerful source of motivation and inspiration, helping us to stay focused and determined in the face of challenges.

Ultimately, believing in our ability to improve is a mindset that can be developed and nurtured over time. By focusing on building our self-efficacy, seeking out feedback, reflecting on our experiences, and surrounding ourselves with a positive support system, we can cultivate a growth mindset that empowers us to achieve our full potential. When we believe in our ability to improve, we open ourselves up to endless possibilities for growth and success. So, embrace the journey of self-improvement with confidence and determination, knowing that you have what it takes to achieve your goals and fulfill your potential.

Chapter 13: Balancing Work and Life

- FINDING HARMONY BETWEEN personal and professional goals

Finding harmony between personal and professional goals is a delicate balance that many individuals strive to achieve. It can be challenging to navigate the demands of work and personal life, but with the right mindset and strategies, it is possible to find a sense of fulfillment and satisfaction in both areas. In this essay, we will explore the importance of aligning personal and professional goals, as well as some tips for achieving harmony between the two.

First and foremost, it is crucial to recognize the interconnected nature of personal and professional goals. Many people tend to compartmentalize their lives, separating their work goals from their personal goals. However, this approach can often lead to feelings of imbalance and dissatisfaction. When personal and professional goals are not aligned, it can create conflict and tension in both areas of life. For example, if someone's personal goal is to spend more time with their family, but their professional goal is to work long hours to climb the corporate ladder, they may find themselves feeling torn between the two. By aligning personal and professional goals, individuals can create a sense of harmony and coherence in their lives.

In order to find harmony between personal and professional goals, it is important to first take the time to reflect on what is truly important to you. This involves examining your values, interests, and aspirations in both your personal and professional life. By gaining a deeper understanding of what you truly want to achieve, you can begin to set goals that are aligned with your values and priorities. For example, if family is a top priority for you, you may choose to set professional goals that allow you to have more flexibility and time to spend with your loved ones. By aligning your personal and professional goals in this way, you can create a sense of balance and fulfillment in both areas of your life.

Another key aspect of finding harmony between personal and professional goals is setting boundaries and prioritizing your time effectively. It can be easy to get caught up in the demands of work and neglect your personal life, or vice versa. By setting clear boundaries and making time for both personal and professional activities, you can ensure that you are meeting your goals in both areas. This may involve setting specific work hours, scheduling regular time for self-care and relaxation, and being mindful of how you are spending your time. By prioritizing your time effectively and setting boundaries, you can create a sense of balance and harmony between your personal and professional goals.

In addition to setting boundaries and prioritizing your time, it is important to also practice self-care and maintain a healthy work-life balance. Taking care of yourself is essential for achieving harmony between personal and professional goals. This may involve engaging in activities that bring you joy and relaxation, such as exercise, hobbies, or spending time with loved ones. By taking care of yourself and prioritizing your well-being, you can ensure that you have the energy and motivation to pursue your goals in both your personal and professional life. Maintaining a healthy work-life balance is key to finding harmony between personal and professional goals.

It is also important to be flexible and adaptable in your approach to achieving personal and professional goals. Life is full of unexpected twists and turns, and it is important to be able to adapt to changes in your circumstances. By staying flexible and open to new opportunities, you can adjust your goals and priorities as needed in order to find harmony between your personal and professional life. This may involve being willing to take risks, try new things, and make changes to your plans as necessary. By approaching your goals with a sense of flexibility and adaptability, you can navigate the complexities of balancing personal and professional aspirations. By aligning your personal and professional goals, setting boundaries, prioritizing your time, practicing self-care, and staying flexible, you can create a sense of balance and fulfillment in both areas of your life. Remember that achieving harmony between personal and professional goals is an ongoing journey, and it is important to be patient with yourself as you navigate the complexities of balancing work and personal life. By staying true to your values and priorities, you can create a sense of coherence and satisfaction in both your personal and professional endeavors.

- Setting boundaries and managing time effectively

Setting boundaries and managing time effectively are essential skills that can greatly impact our overall well-being and productivity. In today's fast-paced world, where we are constantly bombarded with distractions and demands on our time, it is more important than ever to establish clear boundaries and prioritize tasks in order to achieve our goals and maintain a healthy work-life balance. By setting boundaries, we can protect our time and energy, and ensure that we are focusing on what truly matters to us. In this article, we will explore the importance of setting boundaries, strategies for doing so effectively, and tips for managing time efficiently.

One of the key reasons why setting boundaries is crucial is that it allows us to protect our time and energy from being wasted on tasks or activities that do not align with our values or goals. By clearly defining what is important to us and what we are willing to commit to, we can avoid overextending ourselves and feeling overwhelmed. Setting boundaries also helps us to establish a sense of control over our lives, as we are able to make informed decisions about how we spend our time and with whom we choose to engage. This can lead to increased feelings of autonomy and empowerment, which are essential for maintaining a healthy sense of self.

In addition to protecting our time and energy, setting boundaries is also important for maintaining healthy relationships with others. By clearly communicating our limits and expectations, we can avoid misunderstandings and conflicts that can arise when our boundaries are not respected. It is important to note that setting boundaries is not about being selfish or uncooperative, but rather about establishing a framework for healthy interactions and effective communication. When we are able to assert our needs and priorities in a respectful manner, we are more likely to build strong and mutually beneficial relationships with those around us.

There are several strategies that can help us set boundaries effectively. One of the most important steps is to identify our priorities and values, so that we can determine what is truly important to us and where we want to focus our time and energy. This can involve reflecting on our long-term goals, as well as considering our personal and professional values. Once we have a clear understanding of what matters most to us, we can begin to set boundaries around the people, activities, and commitments that align with our priorities.

Another key strategy for setting boundaries is to communicate them clearly and assertively. This can involve setting limits on how much time and energy we are willing to invest in certain tasks or relationships, and being upfront about our needs and expectations. It is important to remember that setting boundaries is not about imposing rules or restrictions on others, but rather about advocating for ourselves and taking ownership of our time and choices. By communicating our boundaries in a respectful and assertive manner, we can ensure that they are understood and respected by those around us.

In addition to setting boundaries, managing time effectively is also essential for achieving our goals and maintaining a healthy work-life balance. Time management involves prioritizing tasks, setting deadlines, and allocating our time in a way that maximizes our productivity and reduces stress. By planning our days and weeks in advance, we can ensure that we are focusing on the most important tasks and making progress towards our goals. This can help us to avoid feeling overwhelmed or scattered, and instead feel in control of our time and responsibilities.

There are several tips that can help us manage our time effectively. One of the most important strategies is to prioritize tasks based on their importance and urgency. This can involve using tools such as to-do lists or priority grids to identify the most critical tasks and allocate our time accordingly. By focusing on the tasks that will have the greatest impact on our goals and well-being, we can ensure that we are making the most of our time and energy.

Another key tip for managing time effectively is to eliminate distractions and minimize interruptions. This can involve setting aside dedicated time for focused work, and creating boundaries around when and how we engage with distractions such as social media or email. By creating a quiet and organized work environment, we can increase our productivity and concentration, and avoid wasting time on unimportant tasks. It is also important to establish boundaries around our availability to others, so that we can protect our time for important tasks and activities. By prioritizing our values and goals, communicating our boundaries clearly, and managing our time wisely, we can increase our productivity and well-being, and create a more fulfilling and balanced life. It is important to remember that setting boundaries and managing time effectively are ongoing processes that require practice and self-awareness, but with dedication and commitment, we can create a more focused and intentional approach to our time and energy.

- Practicing self-care and mindfulness

Self-care and mindfulness are two important practices that can have a profound impact on our overall well-being. In today's fast-paced and often stressful world, it is essential to take the time to prioritize our own health and happiness. By incorporating self-care and mindfulness into our daily routines, we can cultivate a sense of balance, inner peace, and resilience that can help us navigate life's challenges with greater ease.

Self-care is the practice of taking deliberate actions to care for one's physical, emotional, and mental well-being. It involves making choices that prioritize our own needs and ensure that we are giving ourselves the necessary time and attention to recharge and rejuvenate. Self-care can take many forms, from getting enough sleep and eating nutritious foods to engaging in activities that bring us joy and fulfillment. It is not a luxury or indulgence, but rather an essential component of maintaining our health and happiness.

Mindfulness, on the other hand, is the practice of being fully present and engaged in the moment, without judgment or distraction. It involves paying attention to our thoughts, feelings, and sensations with curiosity and openness, rather than allowing them to control us. Mindfulness can be cultivated through practices such as meditation, yoga, and deep breathing exercises, as well as by simply being more aware of our surroundings and how we are feeling in any given moment.

Practicing self-care and mindfulness together can create a powerful synergy that enhances our overall well-being. When we take the time to care for ourselves physically, emotionally, and mentally, we are better able to cultivate the presence and awareness that are essential for mindfulness. Similarly, when we practice mindfulness, we are better able to identify our own needs and prioritize self-care practices that support our health and happiness.

One of the key benefits of practicing self-care and mindfulness is the ability to reduce stress and anxiety. By taking the time to care for ourselves and cultivate mindfulness, we can learn to better manage the inevitable challenges and pressures of daily life. We can develop the skills to recognize when we are feeling overwhelmed or stressed, and to take the necessary steps to relax and recharge. This can have a transformative effect on our overall well-being, helping us to feel more calm, centered, and resilient in the face of adversity.

In addition to reducing stress, practicing self-care and mindfulness can also improve our mental clarity and focus. When we take the time to care for ourselves and practice mindfulness, we are better able to quiet the mind and be fully present in the moment. This can help us to think more clearly, make better decisions, and enhance our creativity and problem-solving abilities. By cultivating a sense of inner peace and clarity through self-care and mindfulness, we can navigate life's challenges with greater ease and confidence.

Another important benefit of practicing self-care and mindfulness is the ability to strengthen our relationships with others. When we take the time to care for ourselves and cultivate mindfulness, we are better able to show up fully for the people in our lives. We can communicate more effectively, listen more attentively, and respond with compassion and understanding. By prioritizing our own well-being and practicing mindfulness, we can create deeper connections with others and cultivate more fulfilling and supportive relationships.

To incorporate self-care and mindfulness into your daily routine, it is important to start small and make gradual changes. Begin by identifying the areas of your life where you could use more self-care, whether it's getting more sleep, eating healthier foods, or making time for activities that bring you joy. Set aside a few minutes each day to practice mindfulness, whether through meditation, deep breathing exercises, or simply by being more present in your daily activities. Over time, you may find that these practices become an essential part of your daily routine, helping you to feel more balanced, centered, and resilient in the face of life's challenges. By prioritizing our own health and happiness, and cultivating the presence and awareness that are essential for mindfulness, we can reduce stress and anxiety, improve mental clarity and focus, strengthen our relationships with others, and navigate life's challenges with greater ease and confidence. By incorporating self-care and mindfulness into our daily routines, we can create a foundation of resilience and well-being that can support us in living a more fulfilling and joyful life.

Chapter 14: Practicing Patience and Persistence

- UNDERSTANDING THE process of goal achievement

Goal achievement is a process that involves setting specific objectives and taking deliberate action to reach them. It is a fundamental aspect of personal and professional development, as it provides direction, motivation, and a sense of accomplishment. In order to effectively achieve goals, one must first establish clear and measurable objectives. These objectives should be realistic and attainable, yet challenging enough to inspire effort and commitment.

Once goals have been set, it is essential to create a concrete plan of action. This plan should outline the steps needed to reach the desired outcome, as well as any potential obstacles that may arise along the way. By breaking down the goal into smaller, manageable tasks, individuals can maintain focus and momentum throughout the process. Additionally, having a clear plan in place can help to monitor progress and make necessary adjustments as needed.

One key component of goal achievement is maintaining a positive mindset. Believing in one's ability to succeed and remaining optimistic in the face of challenges can significantly impact one's motivation and perseverance. Cultivating a growth mindset, which focuses on learning and improvement rather than fixed abilities, can help individuals overcome setbacks and stay committed to their goals. By remaining flexible and adaptable, individuals can adjust their strategies and approaches as needed to stay on track towards success.

In addition to mindset, effective goal achievement also requires effective time management skills. Scheduling dedicated time each day to work towards goals, prioritizing tasks, and eliminating distractions can help individuals stay focused and productive. By setting deadlines and holding oneself accountable, individuals can create a sense of urgency and momentum to propel them towards their desired outcome. It is also important to recognize the importance of self-care and balance, as maintaining a healthy work-life balance can prevent burnout and support overall well-being.

Another critical aspect of goal achievement is the importance of persistence and resilience. Despite the best-laid plans, setbacks and obstacles are inevitable in any pursuit of goals. It is essential for individuals to develop the ability to persevere through challenges and setbacks, remaining committed to their objectives even in the face of adversity. By learning from failures and setbacks, individuals can gain valuable insights and make necessary adjustments to improve their strategies and ultimately achieve success.

Furthermore, goal achievement often involves collaboration and support from others. Building a network of mentors, coaches, and peers can provide valuable guidance, feedback, and encouragement throughout the process. Seeking support from others can help individuals gain new perspectives, access valuable resources, and stay motivated and accountable to their goals. Additionally, celebrating milestones and achievements along the way can help individuals stay motivated and maintain momentum towards their ultimate goal. By setting clear objectives, creating a detailed plan of action, maintaining a positive mindset, managing time effectively, practicing persistence and resilience, and seeking support from others, individuals can increase their likelihood of successfully achieving their goals. Through dedication, hard work, and perseverance, individuals can overcome obstacles, stay committed to their objectives, and ultimately realize their full potential. Goal achievement is a journey that requires dedication, commitment, and effort, but the rewards of success are well worth the investment.

- Embracing the journey, not just the destination

In our fast-paced and goal-oriented society, it is easy to get caught up in the idea that success is solely determined by reaching a specific destination or achieving a particular goal. While it is important to set goals and work towards achieving them, it is equally important to embrace the journey along the way.

The journey is where growth, learning, and self-discovery occurs, and it is often the most rewarding and fulfilling part of the process.

Embracing the journey means savoring every moment, both the highs and the lows, and recognizing that each step taken is a valuable part of the overall experience. It means finding joy in the process of working towards your goals, rather than solely focusing on the end result. By embracing the journey, you allow yourself to be fully present and engaged in the moment, which can lead to a deeper sense of fulfillment and satisfaction.

One of the key benefits of embracing the journey is the opportunity for personal growth and development. As you navigate through challenges, setbacks, and successes, you have the chance to learn more about yourself, your strengths, and your limitations. This self-awareness can lead to increased confidence, resilience, and adaptability, which are essential skills for personal and professional success. The journey also provides opportunities for learning new skills, gaining valuable experiences, and expanding your knowledge and understanding of the world around you.

Furthermore, embracing the journey can lead to a greater sense of gratitude and appreciation for the present moment. When you focus on each step of the journey, rather than getting caught up in the hustle and bustle of everyday life, you can cultivate a greater sense of mindfulness and awareness. This can help you to slow down, be more present, and truly appreciate the beauty and richness of life. Practicing gratitude can also improve your mental and emotional well-being, reduce stress and anxiety, and enhance your overall quality of life.

In addition, embracing the journey can help you to develop a more positive and optimistic mindset. When you focus on the journey, rather than fixating on the end goal, you are more likely to approach challenges and setbacks with a growth mindset. Instead of viewing obstacles as insurmountable barriers, you are more likely to see them as opportunities for learning, growth, and improvement. This can help you to persevere in the face of adversity, stay motivated and determined, and ultimately achieve your goals with a greater sense of fulfillment and satisfaction.

It is important to remember that the journey is where the magic happens. It is where you discover your true potential, overcome obstacles, and experience personal growth and transformation. While reaching your destination is undoubtedly a significant achievement, it is the journey itself that shapes who you are and prepares you for future success. So, the next time you find yourself focused solely on the end goal, take a moment to pause, reflect, and embrace the journey. You may be surprised at the profound impact it can have on your life and your sense of fulfillment and happiness.

- Cultivating patience and resilience

Cultivating patience and resilience is a fundamental aspect of personal development and growth. In today's fast-paced world, it is easy to become overwhelmed by the pressures and demands of daily life. However, by learning to cultivate patience and resilience, individuals can better navigate challenges and setbacks, leading to increased mental strength and emotional well-being. Patience is the ability to tolerate delay, obstacles, or frustration without becoming upset or agitated. It involves maintaining a sense of calm and composure in the face of difficult or challenging situations. Resilience, on the other hand, is the capacity to bounce back from adversity or setbacks. It is the ability to adapt and recover from stressful or traumatic events, emerging stronger and better equipped to face future challenges.

One of the key benefits of cultivating patience and resilience is the ability to manage stress and anxiety effectively. The modern world is filled with stressors, from work deadlines to relationship issues to financial pressures. By developing patience, individuals can better cope with these stressors, maintaining a sense of equilibrium and inner peace even in the face of adversity. Resilience, on the other hand, allows individuals to bounce back from stressful situations, learning from their experiences and building inner strength and fortitude. Together, patience and resilience form a powerful combination that can help individuals navigate the ups and downs of life with greater ease and grace.

Another important benefit of cultivating patience and resilience is the ability to build better relationships with others. The ability to remain patient and calm in challenging situations can help individuals avoid unnecessary conflicts and misunderstandings. By responding with patience and understanding, individuals can foster stronger, more positive relationships with friends, family, and colleagues. Resilience also plays a crucial role in building relationships, as it allows individuals to bounce back from disagreements or conflicts, learning from their experiences and moving forward with a sense of purpose and determination. By cultivating patience and resilience, individuals can create a more harmonious and supportive social network, leading to increased well-being and happiness.

Patience and resilience are also essential qualities for success in both personal and professional endeavors. In the face of setbacks and obstacles, individuals with a strong sense of patience and resilience are better equipped to persevere and achieve their goals. Patience allows individuals to stay focused and determined, even in the face of challenges and setbacks. Resilience, on the other hand, gives individuals the strength and fortitude to bounce back from failures and setbacks, learning from their experiences and moving forward with renewed determination. By cultivating these qualities, individuals can overcome obstacles and achieve their aspirations, leading to greater success and fulfillment in both their personal and professional lives.

There are several strategies that individuals can use to cultivate patience and resilience in their daily lives. One important strategy is practicing mindfulness and meditation. Mindfulness involves staying present and aware in the moment, allowing individuals to respond to challenges with greater clarity and calm. Meditation, on the other hand, can help individuals cultivate inner peace and emotional resilience, reducing stress and anxiety. By incorporating mindfulness and meditation into their daily routine, individuals can develop a greater sense of patience and resilience, better equipping them to face life's challenges with grace and composure.

Another important strategy for cultivating patience and resilience is developing a positive mindset. By focusing on the positive aspects of a situation, individuals can foster a sense of optimism and hope, even in the face of difficulties. This positive mindset can help individuals stay motivated and determined, even when faced with setbacks or obstacles. By reframing negative thoughts and focusing on the potential for growth and learning, individuals can build inner resilience and perseverance. Developing a positive mindset is a powerful tool for cultivating patience and resilience, helping individuals stay strong and resilient in the face of life's challenges. By learning to tolerate delay and adversity with grace and composure, individuals can better navigate life's challenges and setbacks. The ability to bounce back from adversity and setback is essential for building inner strength and fortitude. By incorporating strategies such as mindfulness, meditation, and developing a positive mindset, individuals can cultivate patience and resilience, leading to increased well-being, success, and fulfillment in all areas of life. By embracing these qualities, individuals can move through life with greater ease and grace, approaching challenges with a sense of determination and optimism.

Chapter 15: Adapting to Change

- EMBRACING UNCERTAINTY and change

In today's rapidly evolving world, it is becoming increasingly important for individuals and organizations to embrace uncertainty and change. The pace of technological advancement, globalization, and environmental shifts are reshaping our lives and work in ways that can be unpredictable and unsettling. Rather than resisting these changes, it is essential to adopt a mindset that is open to new possibilities and adaptable to unexpected challenges.

Embracing uncertainty means acknowledging that the future is inherently unknowable and that plans may need to be adjusted as circumstances evolve. It involves letting go of the need for control and instead focusing on being resilient and responsive to whatever comes our way. This approach can be empowering, as it frees us from the constraints of rigid expectations and allows us to tap into our creativity and resourcefulness to address emerging opportunities and threats.

Change is an inevitable part of life, and resisting it can lead to stagnation and missed opportunities. By embracing change, we can position ourselves to thrive in an ever-shifting landscape and to harness the momentum of transformation for our own growth and development. This requires a mindset of curiosity and a willingness to step outside our comfort zone, as well as a commitment to continuous learning and self-improvement.

One key aspect of embracing uncertainty and change is developing emotional intelligence and resilience. This involves cultivating the ability to regulate our emotions, adapt to new situations, and bounce back from setbacks. By building our emotional intelligence, we can navigate uncertainty with greater ease and confidence, maintaining a sense of clarity and purpose even in the face of ambiguity and upheaval.

In addition to emotional intelligence, it is important to cultivate a growth mindset that is oriented towards learning and development. This means viewing challenges as opportunities for growth and seeing setbacks as valuable lessons rather than insurmountable obstacles. By embracing a growth mindset, we can approach uncertainty and change with a sense of optimism and possibility, allowing us to thrive in dynamic and unpredictable environments.

Another crucial aspect of embracing uncertainty and change is fostering a culture of innovation and experimentation. This involves encouraging a spirit of creativity and entrepreneurship, as well as creating a safe space for individuals to take risks and try new approaches. By fostering innovation and experimentation, we can harness the power of diversity and collective intelligence to generate novel solutions to complex problems and to adapt to changing circumstances with agility and resilience.

Ultimately, embracing uncertainty and change requires a holistic approach that balances flexibility and adaptability with a strong sense of purpose and values. It is about finding a middle ground between embracing the unknown and staying grounded in our core beliefs and principles. By adopting a mindset that is open, curious, and resilient, we can navigate uncertainty with confidence and courage, leveraging change as an opportunity for growth and transformation.

- Staying flexible and open-minded

In today's rapidly changing world, the ability to stay flexible and open-minded is more important than ever. With advancements in technology, changes in the workplace, and shifts in societal norms, being able to adapt to new situations and ideas is essential for success. Flexibility and open-mindedness are not only valuable personal traits, but they are also qualities that can benefit organizations, teams, and communities as a whole.

Flexibility can be defined as the willingness to adapt to new circumstances and to consider alternative approaches to solving problems. It involves being able to change course when necessary and to think on your feet in unpredictable situations. Being flexible also means being open to feedback and constructive criticism, and being willing to make adjustments based on new information. Flexible individuals are able to embrace change and uncertainty with a positive attitude, viewing challenges as opportunities for growth and learning.

Open-mindedness, on the other hand, is the willingness to consider different perspectives, ideas, and opinions without automatically dismissing them. It involves being receptive to new information and being willing to reevaluate your own beliefs and assumptions. Open-minded individuals are curious and eager to learn, and they approach discussions and interactions with a sense of curiosity and respect for the diversity of opinions and experiences.

Both flexibility and open-mindedness are closely related and can reinforce each other. Being open-minded can make it easier to be flexible, as it allows you to consider new ideas and perspectives that may lead you to change your plans or adjust your strategies. Similarly, being flexible can help you be more open-minded, as it can make it easier to adapt to new information and take on board the viewpoints of others.

There are several strategies that can help you cultivate and maintain flexibility and open-mindedness in your personal and professional life. One key strategy is to practice mindfulness, which involves being fully present and aware of your thoughts, feelings, and surroundings. By practicing mindfulness, you can become more attuned to new information and more open to different perspectives, which can help you stay flexible and open-minded in the face of change.

Another important strategy is to seek out diverse perspectives and experiences. This can involve engaging in conversations with people who have different backgrounds and viewpoints, reading books and articles that challenge your beliefs, and seeking out new experiences that push you outside of your comfort zone. By exposing yourself to new ideas and perspectives, you can broaden your horizons and become more open-minded.

It is also important to cultivate a growth mindset, which involves viewing challenges and setbacks as opportunities for learning and growth. By adopting a growth mindset, you can approach new situations with a positive attitude and a willingness to learn from your experiences. This can help you stay flexible and open-minded, as it can make it easier to adapt to change and to consider new ideas and perspectives. By cultivating these qualities in ourselves and in our organizations, we can better navigate the challenges and opportunities that come our way. Flexibility and open-mindedness are not only valuable personal traits, but they are also qualities that can enhance collaboration, innovation, and success in all areas of life. So let us embrace change, seek out new perspectives, and approach challenges with a sense of curiosity and open-mindedness.

- Using change as an opportunity for growth

Change is an inevitable part of life that can often be met with resistance and fear. However, it is important to recognize that change can also present opportunities for growth and development. By embracing change and seeing it as a chance to learn and improve, individuals can harness its potential to transform their lives in positive ways.

One key aspect of using change as an opportunity for growth is having a growth mindset. This means approaching change with an open and optimistic attitude, believing that challenges and setbacks are opportunities for learning and personal development. By viewing change as a chance to expand one's abilities and skills, individuals can adapt more easily and navigate through transitions with greater resilience and confidence.

In addition to having a growth mindset, it is also important to be proactive in seeking out opportunities for growth during times of change. This may involve taking on new challenges, exploring different paths, or learning new skills. By actively seeking ways to grow and develop during times of transition, individuals can make the most of the opportunities that change presents and come out stronger on the other side.

Furthermore, using change as an opportunity for growth requires a willingness to step outside of one's comfort zone and embrace uncertainty. It is natural to feel anxious or apprehensive in the face of change, but by pushing oneself to try new things and take risks, individuals can expand their comfort zone and discover new strengths and capabilities. By embracing the unknown and being open to new experiences, individuals can cultivate a sense of curiosity and resilience that can help them grow and thrive in the face of change.

Another important aspect of using change as an opportunity for growth is maintaining a sense of perspective and focusing on the bigger picture. During times of change, it can be easy to get caught up in the immediate challenges and obstacles, but by keeping sight of long-term goals and aspirations, individuals can see change as a stepping stone towards personal and professional growth. By staying focused on the positive outcomes that can result from change, individuals can maintain motivation and momentum in their journey towards personal development and growth. By approaching change with an open and optimistic attitude, seeking out opportunities for growth, stepping outside of one's comfort zone, and maintaining perspective, individuals can harness the transformative power of change to propel themselves towards growth and development. Embracing change as a chance to learn, adapt, and evolve can lead to personal and professional growth that can enrich one's life in profound ways.

Chapter 16: Building Healthy Habits

- INCORPORATING POSITIVE habits into daily routines

Developing positive habits and incorporating them into daily routines can have a significant impact on our overall well-being and productivity. Whether it's something as simple as starting our day with a morning meditation or making sure to drink enough water throughout the day, implementing these habits can help us lead a more balanced and fulfilling life. In this article, we will explore the importance of positive habits, how to identify which habits to focus on, and practical strategies for successfully integrating them into our daily routines.

One of the key benefits of incorporating positive habits into our daily routines is the impact they can have on our mental and emotional well-being. For example, practicing gratitude daily can help shift our mindset towards a more positive outlook on life, while regular exercise can boost our mood and energy levels. By making these habits a part of our everyday life, we can cultivate a more resilient mindset and better cope with stress and challenges that come our way.

Another important aspect of positive habits is their ability to improve our physical health. For example, getting an adequate amount of sleep each night and eating a balanced diet can have a significant impact on our overall health and well-being. By incorporating these habits into our daily routines, we can reduce our risk of chronic diseases, improve our immune function, and increase our overall longevity.

When it comes to identifying which habits to focus on, it's important to consider our personal goals and values. Think about what areas of your life you would like to improve and what habits can help you achieve those goals. For example, if you want to improve your productivity at work, you may consider incorporating habits such as time-blocking or setting daily goals. If you want to improve your physical health, you may focus on habits such as regular exercise, healthy eating, and staying hydrated.

Once you have identified which habits to focus on, it's important to create a plan for incorporating them into your daily routine. Start by setting specific and achievable goals for each habit. For example, if you want to start a daily meditation practice, you may start with just five minutes a day and gradually increase the time as you become more comfortable with the practice. It's also helpful to create reminders or cues for yourself to help you remember to engage in these habits. For example, you can set a daily alarm on your phone or place sticky notes around your home as reminders.

In addition to setting goals and creating reminders, it's important to track your progress and hold yourself accountable. Keep a journal or use a habit-tracking app to monitor your consistency and progress with each habit. This can help you stay motivated and identify any patterns or obstacles that may be preventing you from successfully incorporating these habits into your daily routine.

Lastly, it's important to be patient and kind to yourself as you work on incorporating positive habits into your daily routine. Change takes time, and it's normal to experience setbacks or struggles along the way. Remember that developing positive habits is a journey, not a destination, and every small step you take towards improving your habits is a win. Celebrate your successes, no matter how small, and be gentle with yourself when you encounter challenges. With dedication, patience, and a positive attitude, you can successfully integrate these habits into your daily routine and reap the benefits of a healthier and more fulfilling life.

- Breaking bad habits

Breaking bad habits can be a challenging and daunting task for many individuals. Whether it's biting your nails, overeating, or procrastinating, bad habits can have a negative impact on both our physical and mental well-being. However, with the right strategies and mindset, it is possible to overcome these habits and make positive changes in our lives.

One of the first steps in breaking a bad habit is to identify the underlying cause. Bad habits are often a result of underlying emotional or psychological issues, such as stress, anxiety, or low self-esteem. By understanding the root cause of your habit, you can begin to address the underlying issues and make lasting changes. For example, if you tend to overeat when you are feeling stressed, you may need to find healthier ways to cope with stress, such as practicing mindfulness or engaging in physical activity.

Once you have identified the root cause of your bad habit, it is important to set specific and achievable goals for breaking the habit. It can be overwhelming to try to completely eliminate a bad habit all at once, so setting smaller, achievable goals can help you make gradual progress towards breaking the habit. For example, if you have a habit of procrastinating, you could set a goal to work on a task for 15 minutes each day before taking a break. Breaking the habit into smaller tasks can make it more manageable and increase your chances of success.

Another important factor in breaking bad habits is creating a supportive environment. Surrounding yourself with people who support your goals and can help hold you accountable can greatly increase your chances of success. Additionally, removing triggers or temptations that may lead to the habit can help you stay on track. For example, if you have a habit of smoking, you may need to avoid places where smoking is allowed or find alternative coping mechanisms for stress.

In addition to creating a supportive environment, it is important to replace bad habits with healthier alternatives. Breaking a bad habit is not only about stopping the behavior, but also about finding healthier ways to meet your needs. For example, if you have a habit of overeating, you could find other ways to cope with stress or boredom, such as going for a walk or practicing relaxation techniques. By replacing the bad habit with a healthier alternative, you can create lasting changes in your behavior.

Changing a habit takes time and effort, so it is important to be patient and kind to yourself throughout the process. It is normal to experience setbacks or slip-ups along the way, but it is important to learn from these moments and continue to move forward. Remember that breaking a bad habit is a journey, not a destination, and that progress is more important than perfection. Celebrate your successes, no matter how small, and keep pushing yourself towards your goals. By identifying the root cause of your habit, setting specific goals, creating a supportive environment, replacing bad habits with healthier alternatives, and being patient and kind to yourself, you can make lasting changes in your behavior. Remember that breaking a bad habit is a journey, and that progress is more important than perfection. With dedication and effort, you can overcome your bad habits and create a healthier, happier life for yourself.

- Creating a supportive environment for success

Creating a supportive environment for success is crucial for individuals to thrive and reach their full potential. Whether in the workplace, classroom, or any other setting, a supportive environment is essential for fostering motivation, collaboration, and productivity. In order to create such an environment, it is important to consider various factors such as communication, trust, recognition, and accountability.

Effective communication is one of the key elements in creating a supportive environment for success. Clear and open communication helps build trust among team members, reduces misunderstandings, and promotes a sense of belonging and inclusion. In order to foster effective communication, it is important for leaders to establish open channels of communication, encourage feedback, and actively listen to the concerns and ideas of others. By promoting a culture of transparency and honesty, individuals are more likely to feel supported and empowered to express themselves.

Trust is another essential component of a supportive environment. Trust is the foundation of successful relationships, whether between colleagues, employees, or students. When individuals trust each other, they are more likely to collaborate effectively, take risks, and support each other in achieving common goals. Building trust takes time and effort, but it is well worth the investment. Leaders can cultivate trust by demonstrating integrity, keeping commitments, and empowering others to make decisions and take ownership of their work.

Recognition and appreciation are also important aspects of creating a supportive environment for success. Recognizing and celebrating the achievements and contributions of individuals not only boosts morale and motivation but also reinforces positive behavior and performance. By acknowledging the efforts and accomplishments of team members, leaders can inspire a culture of excellence and encourage others to strive for their best. Simple gestures of recognition, such as a thank-you note or public acknowledgment, can go a long way in fostering a supportive and positive environment.

Accountability is another essential factor in creating a supportive environment for success. Accountability involves taking responsibility for one's actions, meeting commitments, and holding oneself and others to high standards. In a supportive environment, individuals feel encouraged to take ownership of their work, set goals, and strive for excellence. By establishing clear expectations, providing feedback, and holding individuals accountable for their performance, leaders can create a culture of accountability that promotes growth and success. By fostering a culture of openness, trust, appreciation, and responsibility, leaders can empower individuals to reach their full potential and achieve their goals. A supportive environment not only promotes collaboration and productivity but also enhances morale, motivation, and overall well-being. By investing in building a supportive environment, organizations can create a positive and thriving workplace or academic setting where individuals can excel and succeed.

Chapter 17: Cultivating Confidence and Self-belief

- BUILDING SELF-ESTEEM and confidence

Self-esteem and confidence play crucial roles in one's overall well-being and success in life. Both concepts are interconnected, as having a high level of self-esteem often translates into greater self-confidence, and vice versa. Self-esteem refers to how individuals perceive and value themselves, while confidence is the belief in one's abilities to succeed in various tasks and challenges. Building and maintaining healthy levels of self-esteem and confidence are essential for personal growth, resilience, and overall happiness.

There are various factors that can influence an individual's self-esteem and confidence levels. One of the most significant factors is childhood experiences, such as family dynamics, school environment, and societal expectations. Negative experiences, such as bullying, criticism, or neglect, can have a lasting impact on a person's self-perception and confidence. On the other hand, positive experiences, such as validation, support, and encouragement, can contribute to the development of healthy self-esteem and confidence.

In addition to childhood experiences, personal qualities and beliefs also play a significant role in shaping self-esteem and confidence. Individuals who possess qualities such as resilience, optimism, and self-awareness are more likely to have higher levels of self-esteem and confidence. Beliefs about one's abilities, worth, and potential also contribute to self-esteem and confidence. Those who believe in themselves and their abilities are more likely to take risks, pursue their goals, and overcome challenges with resilience and determination.

Building self-esteem and confidence is a lifelong process that requires self-reflection, self-compassion, and personal growth. It is essential to practice self-awareness and mindfulness to understand one's thoughts, feelings, and behaviors. By becoming aware of negative self-talk, limiting beliefs, and self-sabotaging behaviors, individuals can start to challenge and change them. Self-compassion is also crucial in building self-esteem and confidence. By treating oneself with kindness, understanding, and acceptance, individuals can cultivate a positive self-image and sense of worth.

Setting realistic goals and taking action towards achieving them is another important strategy for building self-esteem and confidence. By setting achievable goals, individuals can experience a sense of accomplishment and success, which can boost their self-esteem and confidence. Taking small steps towards goals, celebrating achievements, and learning from setbacks are all part of the process of building self-esteem and confidence. Additionally, seeking support from friends, family, mentors, or mental health professionals can also be beneficial in building self-esteem and confidence. Having a support system can provide encouragement, feedback, and perspective, which can help individuals navigate challenges and setbacks with resilience and determination. By understanding the factors that influence self-esteem and confidence, practicing self-awareness and self-compassion, setting realistic goals, taking action, and seeking support, individuals can cultivate healthy levels of self-esteem and confidence. It is a lifelong journey that requires patience, self-reflection, and personal growth. By investing in building self-esteem and confidence, individuals can increase their resilience, pursue their goals, and lead happier and more fulfilling lives.

- Overcoming self-doubt and imposter syndrome

Self-doubt and imposter syndrome are common challenges that many individuals face in their personal and professional lives. These feelings of inadequacy and self-doubt can be crippling, preventing individuals from achieving their full potential and hindering their success. It is important to recognize and address these feelings in order to overcome them and move forward with confidence and self-assurance.

One of the first steps in overcoming self-doubt and imposter syndrome is to acknowledge and accept that these feelings are normal and that many people experience them at some point in their lives. It is important to understand that these feelings are often rooted in fear and insecurity, and that they do not necessarily reflect reality or a person's true capabilities. By recognizing that self-doubt is a common experience, individuals can begin to take steps to address and overcome these feelings.

One effective way to combat self-doubt and imposter syndrome is to practice self-compassion and self-acceptance. This involves being kind and forgiving to oneself, and recognizing that it is okay to have moments of self-doubt or insecurity. By practicing self-compassion, individuals can learn to treat themselves with the same level of care and understanding that they would offer to a friend in a similar situation. This can help to alleviate feelings of inadequacy and build self-confidence and self-assurance.

Another important strategy for overcoming self-doubt and imposter syndrome is to challenge negative self-talk and limiting beliefs. Many individuals tend to engage in negative self-talk, such as telling themselves that they are not good enough or that they do not deserve success. These beliefs can be deeply ingrained and difficult to overcome, but it is possible to challenge and change them with practice and perseverance. By replacing negative self-talk with positive affirmations and reframing limiting beliefs, individuals can begin to build a more positive and empowering mindset.

It is also helpful to seek support from others when facing self-doubt and imposter syndrome. Talking to friends, family, or a therapist about these feelings can provide valuable perspective and reassurance, and can help individuals to gain a better understanding of their own worth and abilities. Surrounding oneself with a supportive community of individuals who believe in and encourage them can make a significant difference in overcoming self-doubt and building self-confidence.

In addition to seeking support from others, it can be beneficial to practice self-care and prioritize one's well-being. Taking care of oneself physically, emotionally, and mentally can help individuals to feel more grounded and resilient in the face of self-doubt and imposter syndrome. This can involve engaging in activities that bring joy and relaxation, such as exercise, meditation, or spending time with loved ones. By prioritizing self-care, individuals can nurture their sense of self-worth and strengthen their ability to overcome self-doubt.

In short, it is important for individuals struggling with self-doubt and imposter syndrome to set realistic goals and expectations for themselves. Perfectionism and setting unattainable standards can fuel feelings of inadequacy and self-doubt, so it is important to be gentle with oneself and celebrate accomplishments, no matter how small. By setting achievable goals and recognizing one's efforts and progress, individuals can build confidence and self-esteem, and begin to overcome self-doubt and imposter syndrome. By acknowledging and accepting these feelings, practicing self-compassion and self-acceptance, challenging negative self-talk and limiting beliefs, seeking support from others, prioritizing self-care, and setting realistic goals, individuals can begin to combat self-doubt and build self-confidence. With determination and perseverance, it is possible to overcome self-doubt and imposter syndrome and achieve one's full potential.

- Setting boundaries and advocating for yourself

Setting boundaries and advocating for yourself are crucial skills that can greatly impact your personal and professional life. Boundaries are guidelines or limits that a person creates to identify acceptable behaviors from others. These boundaries can be physical, emotional, or mental, and are essential for maintaining healthy relationships and ensuring your well-being. Advocating for yourself involves speaking up for your needs and wants, standing up for your rights, and asserting yourself in various situations. By setting boundaries and advocating for yourself, you can assert your worth, protect yourself from manipulation or exploitation, and create a more positive and fulfilling life.

One of the key benefits of setting boundaries is the ability to protect your mental and emotional well-being. Without clear boundaries, you may find yourself feeling overwhelmed, stressed, or resentful in relationships or situations where your needs are not being met. By establishing boundaries, you can create a sense of safety and security for yourself, ensuring that others respect your limits and treat you with the courtesy and consideration you deserve. Setting boundaries can also improve your self-esteem and self-confidence, as you assert your worth and value by advocating for what is important to you.

In addition to protecting your mental and emotional well-being, setting boundaries can also help you maintain healthy relationships with others.

Boundaries provide a framework for healthy communication and interaction, allowing for mutual respect and understanding between individuals. By clearly defining your boundaries, you can prevent misunderstandings or conflicts from arising and promote harmony and cooperation in your relationships. Setting boundaries can also help you establish fair and balanced dynamics in your interactions with others, ensuring that your needs are met and that you are not taken advantage of or mistreated.

Advocating for yourself goes hand in hand with setting boundaries, as it involves asserting your needs and wants in various situations. Advocating for yourself is about standing up for your rights, communicating your needs and desires clearly, and taking action to ensure that your interests are represented and respected. By advocating for yourself, you can assert your independence, autonomy, and agency in your personal and professional life, demonstrating that you are capable of taking care of yourself and making decisions that align with your values and goals.

One of the key aspects of advocating for yourself is effective communication. Being able to clearly and assertively communicate your needs, boundaries, and expectations is essential for advocating for yourself in various situations. This requires being able to express yourself in a confident and respectful manner, using assertive communication techniques such as "I" statements, setting clear expectations, and following through on your commitments. By mastering effective communication skills, you can ensure that your voice is heard, your needs are met, and your boundaries are respected in all aspects of your life.

Advocating for yourself also involves developing a strong sense of self-awareness and self-advocacy. This means knowing yourself well, understanding your values, beliefs, and priorities, and being able to assert them confidently and assertively in various situations. Self-awareness is essential for advocating for yourself, as it allows you to identify your needs and desires, set boundaries that align with your values, and communicate your expectations effectively. By developing self-awareness and self-advocacy, you can cultivate a sense of empowerment and agency in your life, taking control of your own destiny and steering it in a direction that reflects your true self and aspirations.

In addition to effective communication and self-awareness, advocating for yourself also requires developing healthy assertiveness skills. Assertiveness is the ability to express your needs and wants confidently and directly, without being passive or aggressive. Assertive communication involves speaking up for yourself, setting boundaries, and standing up for your rights in a respectful and firm manner, while also listening to others and considering their perspectives. By practicing assertiveness skills, you can assert your worth and assert your boundaries in various situations, ensuring that your needs are met and that you are treated with the respect and consideration you deserve.

Furthermore, advocating for yourself involves taking action and being proactive in seeking out opportunities to assert your needs and desires. This may involve speaking up in meetings, negotiating for a raise or promotion, setting boundaries with friends or family members, or advocating for your rights in various social or political contexts. By taking a proactive approach to advocating for yourself, you can assert your agency and autonomy, and demonstrate to others that you are capable of standing up for yourself and achieving your goals. Being proactive in advocating for yourself also means being willing to take risks, step out of your comfort zone, and assert yourself in challenging or uncomfortable situations, in order to create positive change and improve your life. By setting boundaries, you can protect your mental and emotional well-being, maintain healthy relationships, and assert your worth and value in various situations. Advocating for yourself involves speaking up for your needs and wants, asserting your rights, and taking action to ensure that your interests are represented and respected. By mastering effective communication, self-awareness, assertiveness, and proactive action, you can cultivate a strong sense of self-advocacy and assertiveness, and create a more positive and fulfilling life for yourself. Remember to prioritize self-care and self-compassion as you navigate the process of setting boundaries and advocating for yourself, and always remember that your voice matters and deserves to be heard.

Chapter 18: Managing Stress and Well-being

- COPING WITH STRESS and anxiety

Stress and anxiety are common experiences that many people face on a daily basis, and they can have a significant impact on our mental and physical well-being. Coping with stress and anxiety is essential for maintaining a healthy and balanced life, and there are several strategies that can be helpful in managing these emotions effectively.

One of the key strategies for coping with stress and anxiety is to practice mindfulness and relaxation techniques. Mindfulness involves being present in the moment and paying attention to your thoughts and emotions without judgment. By practicing mindfulness, you can learn to acknowledge and accept your feelings without becoming overwhelmed by them. Relaxation techniques, such as deep breathing exercises, progressive muscle relaxation, and guided imagery, can also help to calm the mind and body and reduce feelings of stress and anxiety.

Another important aspect of coping with stress and anxiety is maintaining a healthy lifestyle. This includes eating a balanced diet, getting regular exercise, and getting an adequate amount of sleep each night. Eating a healthy diet rich in fruits, vegetables, whole grains, and lean proteins can help to support your overall well-being and reduce feelings of stress and anxiety. Regular exercise has been shown to have a positive impact on mental health by reducing stress hormones and increasing endorphins, which are natural mood-boosting chemicals in the brain. Additionally, getting enough sleep is essential for maintaining optimal mental and emotional health, as sleep deprivation can exacerbate feelings of stress and anxiety.

In addition to mindfulness and relaxation techniques and maintaining a healthy lifestyle, it can be helpful to engage in activities that bring you joy and fulfillment. Pursuing hobbies, spending time with loved ones, and participating in social activities can all help to distract your mind from stress and anxiety and provide a sense of purpose and fulfillment. Engaging in activities that you enjoy can also help to boost your mood and increase your overall sense of well-being.

It is also important to reach out for support when coping with stress and anxiety. Talking to a trusted friend, family member, or mental health professional can provide you with much-needed support and guidance during challenging times. Support groups and therapy can also be helpful in providing coping strategies and tools for managing stress and anxiety effectively. Remember that it is okay to ask for help when you need it, and seeking support is a sign of strength, not weakness. By practicing mindfulness and relaxation techniques, maintaining a healthy lifestyle, engaging in activities that bring you joy, and reaching out for support, you can effectively manage your stress and anxiety and improve your overall well-being. Remember that it is okay to put yourself and your mental health first, and taking proactive steps to cope with stress and anxiety is a positive and empowering choice.

- Practicing self-care and relaxation techniques

Self-care and relaxation techniques are essential components of maintaining overall well-being and managing stress in our busy lives. In today's fast-paced world, it is easy to neglect our own mental and physical health in favor of meeting the demands of work, school, or family responsibilities. However, the importance of carving out time for self-care should not be underestimated. By taking the time to practice relaxation techniques and engage in activities that promote self-care, we can improve our mood, reduce anxiety, and enhance our overall quality of life.

One of the key aspects of practicing self-care is recognizing the signs of stress and knowing when to take a step back and prioritize our own well-being. It is important to listen to our bodies and minds when they are telling us that we need a break. This could manifest as physical symptoms such as headaches, stomachaches, or muscle tension, or as emotional symptoms like irritability, mood swings, or feelings of overwhelm. By being attuned to these signs, we can intervene early and prevent stress from escalating to the point where it becomes debilitating.

Once we have identified that we are in need of self-care, it is important to take proactive steps to address our stress and promote relaxation. There are a variety of techniques that can be effective in promoting relaxation and reducing stress, and it is important to find what works best for you. Some people may find solace in activities such as meditation, deep breathing exercises, or yoga, while others may prefer engaging in physical activity, spending time in nature, or practicing mindfulness. The key is to experiment with different techniques and find what resonates with you personally.

In addition to individual relaxation techniques, it can also be beneficial to engage in activities that promote overall well-being and self-care. This could include spending time with loved ones, indulging in hobbies that bring joy and fulfillment, or seeking out professional help through therapy or counseling. Taking care of our mental and emotional health is just as important as tending to our physical well-being, and seeking support from others can be a crucial aspect of maintaining overall wellness.

Self-care is not a one-size-fits-all solution, and it is important to tailor our self-care practices to our own unique needs and preferences. What works for one person may not work for another, and it is important to be open to exploring different techniques and approaches to find what resonates with you personally. It is also important to be patient with yourself and to recognize that self-care is a journey, not a destination. It takes time and effort to cultivate a self-care routine that works for you, and it is okay to experiment and make adjustments along the way.

Ultimately, practicing self-care and relaxation techniques is an essential aspect of maintaining overall well-being and managing stress in our busy lives. By prioritizing our own mental and physical health, we can improve our mood, reduce anxiety, and enhance our overall quality of life. It is important to listen to our bodies and minds, to recognize the signs of stress, and to take proactive steps to address our needs. By engaging in activities that promote relaxation and self-care, we can cultivate a sense of balance and resilience that will serve us well in the face of life's challenges.

- **Prioritizing mental and emotional well-being**

The importance of prioritizing mental and emotional well-being cannot be overstated in today's fast-paced and demanding world. With the constant pressure to excel in our personal and professional lives, it is all too easy to neglect our own mental and emotional health. However, the reality is that neglecting these aspects of our well-being can have serious consequences in the long run.

Research has shown that mental and emotional well-being play a crucial role in our overall health and quality of life. Poor mental health has been linked to a range of physical health problems, including heart disease, diabetes, and even cancer. In addition, emotional well-being is closely tied to our ability to form and maintain meaningful relationships, as well as our capacity for resilience in the face of adversity.

It is therefore essential to prioritize mental and emotional well-being in order to live a fulfilling and healthy life. This can be achieved through a variety of practices and strategies that promote mental and emotional wellness. For example, practicing mindfulness and meditation can help reduce stress and anxiety, improve focus and concentration, and cultivate a sense of inner peace and well-being.

In addition, engaging in regular physical activity has been shown to have a positive impact on mental health, as it can help boost mood, reduce symptoms of depression and anxiety, and improve overall mental well-being. Eating a balanced diet rich in fruits, vegetables, whole grains, and lean proteins can also have a positive effect on mental and emotional health, as certain nutrients have been linked to improved mood and cognitive function.

Another important aspect of prioritizing mental and emotional well-being is seeking support from others. Whether through professional therapy, support groups, or simply talking to loved ones, it is important to reach out for help when feeling overwhelmed or struggling with emotional issues. Building a strong support network can provide a source of comfort, encouragement, and guidance during challenging times. By taking proactive steps to care for our mental and emotional health, we can improve our overall well-being, enhance our relationships, and increase our resilience in the face of life's challenges.

Remember, it is okay to prioritize your mental and emotional well-being, and doing so will ultimately benefit not only yourself but those around you as well.

92

Chapter 19: Reflecting on Your Journey

- LOOKING BACK ON ACHIEVEMENTS and failures

Reflecting on achievements and failures is a crucial aspect of personal and professional growth. It allows individuals to assess their progress, identify strengths and weaknesses, and make informed decisions moving forward. By acknowledging both the successes and setbacks experienced along the way, individuals can gain valuable insights that can help them navigate future challenges more effectively.

When looking back on achievements, it is important to celebrate the milestones and accomplishments that have been reached. Whether it be a successful project completion, a promotion at work, or a personal goal achieved, recognizing these accomplishments can boost confidence and motivation. By acknowledging the hard work and dedication that went into achieving these goals, individuals can build a sense of pride and fulfillment in their efforts.

On the other hand, reflecting on failures can be a challenging but equally important exercise. Failures are not indicators of personal worth or ability, but rather opportunities for growth and learning. By examining the reasons for failure, individuals can identify areas for improvement and develop strategies for overcoming obstacles in the future. It is through failure that individuals can gain valuable insights and refine their skills, ultimately leading to greater success in the long run.

It is also important to consider the role of external factors in both achievements and failures. While personal effort and determination play a significant role in individual success, external factors such as luck, timing, and support systems also play a part. By recognizing the influence of these external factors, individuals can gain a more balanced perspective on their achievements and failures and avoid placing undue blame or taking sole credit for outcomes.

Looking back on achievements and failures can also provide valuable context for future decision-making. By understanding what has worked well in the past and what has not, individuals can make more informed choices about their goals, priorities, and strategies moving forward. This reflective process can help individuals set realistic expectations, anticipate potential challenges, and develop effective plans for achieving their desired outcomes. By celebrating successes, learning from failures, and considering the role of external factors, individuals can gain valuable insights that can inform their future decisions and actions. This process of self-reflection and evaluation can lead to greater self-awareness, resilience, and ultimately, success in achieving personal and professional goals.

- Identifying lessons learned

Identifying lessons learned is a crucial step in the process of continuous improvement and development within any organization. By reflecting on past experiences and evaluating what worked well and what didn't, teams can gain valuable insights that can inform future decisions and actions.

One key aspect of identifying lessons learned is the importance of creating a culture that values reflection and feedback. This means encouraging team members to openly discuss their experiences, both positive and negative, and to learn from them. It also involves fostering a sense of trust and psychological safety within the team so that individuals feel comfortable sharing their thoughts and experiences without fear of judgment or reprisal. By creating a safe space for open and honest communication, teams can more effectively identify and learn from their mistakes, leading to stronger performance and outcomes in the future.

Another critical element of identifying lessons learned is the process of documentation and analysis. In order to truly understand and extract insights from past experiences, it is essential to document key information, such as the context, actions taken, outcomes, and lessons learned. This documentation serves as a valuable resource for future reference and can help to identify patterns, trends, and areas for improvement. By conducting a thorough analysis of past experiences, teams can uncover valuable insights that can inform their decision-making and actions in the future, ultimately leading to more effective and efficient performance.

In addition to documenting and analyzing past experiences, it is also important to actively seek out feedback from others. This can include seeking input from colleagues, stakeholders, customers, or other relevant parties who may have valuable perspectives to offer. By soliciting feedback from a variety of sources, teams can gain a more comprehensive understanding of their experiences and potential lessons learned. This external perspective can help to challenge assumptions, highlight blind spots, and provide valuable insights that may have otherwise been overlooked.

Furthermore, identifying lessons learned also involves a commitment to continuous improvement and learning. This means actively seeking out opportunities for growth and development, both individually and as a team. By adopting a growth mindset and a willingness to learn from past experiences, teams can create a culture of innovation and adaptation that will help them thrive in an ever-changing environment. This requires a willingness to experiment, take risks, and embrace change, even in the face of uncertainty. By continuously seeking to improve and learn, teams can stay ahead of the curve and adapt more effectively to new challenges and opportunities. By creating a culture that values reflection and feedback, documenting and analyzing past experiences, seeking out external perspectives, and committing to continuous improvement, teams can gain valuable insights that can inform their decision-making and actions in the future. This process not only leads to more effective and efficient performance but also fosters a culture of innovation and adaptability that will help organizations thrive in an ever-changing world. By embracing the practice of identifying lessons learned, organizations can position themselves for long-term success and sustainability.

- Setting intentions for the future

Setting intentions for the future is an important aspect of personal and professional development. By taking the time to reflect on our goals and aspirations, we can create a roadmap for achieving success and fulfillment in the years to come. Setting intentions involves identifying what we want to achieve, why it is important to us, and how we plan to make it happen. By setting clear intentions, we can stay focused, motivated, and on track to reach our desired outcomes.

One of the first steps in setting intentions for the future is to take stock of our current situation and assess where we stand in relation to our goals. This may involve reflecting on our values, strengths, weaknesses, and areas for growth. By understanding ourselves better, we can set intentions that are aligned with our values, passions, and desires. This self-awareness can help us set realistic and meaningful goals that are relevant to our personal and professional aspirations.

Once we have a clear understanding of where we are and where we want to go, we can begin to set specific intentions for the future. These intentions should be challenging yet achievable, and should be framed in a positive and affirming way. For example, instead of setting an intention to "lose weight," we might frame our intention as "to prioritize my health and wellness by exercising regularly and eating nutritious foods. " By setting intentions that are positive, specific, and actionable, we can create a clear path forward and stay motivated to achieve our desired outcomes.

In addition to setting specific intentions, it is important to also set timelines and milestones to track our progress towards our goals. By breaking down our intentions into smaller, manageable steps, we can create a sense of momentum and achievement as we work towards our larger aspirations. Setting timelines and milestones can also help us stay accountable to our intentions and make adjustments as needed to stay on track.

Another important aspect of setting intentions for the future is to regularly review and revise our goals as needed. As we grow and evolve, our priorities and aspirations may change, and it is important to be flexible and open to reassessing our intentions as needed. By regularly reviewing our goals and progress, we can ensure that our intentions remain relevant, meaningful, and achievable as we continue to work towards our desired outcomes. By taking the time to reflect on our goals, values, and aspirations, we can create a clear roadmap for achieving our desired outcomes. By setting specific, challenging, and positive intentions, creating timelines and milestones, and regularly reviewing and revising our goals, we can stay focused, motivated, and on track to reach our full potential. Whether it is in our personal relationships, career, health, or other areas of our lives, setting intentions for the future can help us create the life we truly want and deserve.

Chapter 20: Conclusion

- RECAP OF KEY TAKEAWAYS from the User Manual

In reviewing the user manual, it is essential to highlight the key takeaways that have been outlined in the document. The user manual serves as a valuable resource for individuals seeking to understand how to utilize a particular product or service effectively. It provides detailed instructions on how to use the product, troubleshoot common issues, and maximize its capabilities. By summarizing the key points from the user manual, users can quickly grasp the essential information needed to get the most out of the product.

One of the primary takeaways from the user manual is the importance of familiarizing oneself with the product's features and functions. This includes understanding how the product operates, what its capabilities are, and how to navigate its interface. By taking the time to read through the user manual thoroughly, users can gain a clear understanding of how to use the product effectively and avoid any potential pitfalls that may arise from improper use.

Additionally, the user manual provides valuable information on troubleshooting common issues that users may encounter while using the product. This includes guidance on how to address technical difficulties, resolve software glitches, and perform maintenance tasks to keep the product running smoothly. By following the troubleshooting steps outlined in the user manual, users can effectively address any problems that may arise and prevent them from escalating further.

Another key takeaway from the user manual is the importance of following safety guidelines and best practices when using the product. This includes understanding how to properly handle the product, store it safely, and maintain it in good working condition. By adhering to the safety recommendations provided in the user manual, users can prevent accidents, injuries, and damage to the product, ensuring a safe and enjoyable user experience.

Furthermore, the user manual highlights the importance of regular software updates and maintenance to ensure optimal performance of the product. By downloading the latest software updates and following the maintenance guidelines outlined in the user manual, users can keep the product functioning at its best and avoid any potential issues that may arise from outdated software or neglecting maintenance tasks. By reviewing the key takeaways outlined in the user manual, users can gain a clear understanding of how to use the product effectively, troubleshoot common issues, follow safety guidelines, and maintain the product for optimal performance. By following the recommendations provided in the user manual, users can ensure a positive user experience and get the most out of the product.

- Encouragement to continue charting your course towards success

Many individuals find themselves at a crossroads in their journey towards success, unsure of whether they should continue on their current path or change course. This uncertainty is natural and can be attributed to a variety of factors such as fear of failure, societal expectations, or self-doubt. However, it is essential to remember that success is not linear and everyone's path is unique to them. By charting your course towards success and staying true to your goals and aspirations, you are taking important steps towards achieving your dreams.

One key aspect of charting your course towards success is to set clear and achievable goals for yourself. These goals should be specific, measurable, attainable, relevant, and time-bound, also known as SMART goals. By clearly defining what you want to achieve and when you want to achieve it by, you are setting yourself up for success and giving yourself a roadmap to follow. Additionally, breaking down your goals into smaller, more manageable tasks can help you stay motivated and focused as you work towards your larger objectives.

Another important aspect of charting your course towards success is to surround yourself with a supportive network of individuals who believe in you and your abilities. Whether it be friends, family, mentors, or colleagues, having a strong support system can make all the difference in achieving your goals. These individuals can provide encouragement, guidance, and advice when you need it most, as well as offer a different perspective on your journey towards success. Remember, success is not a solo endeavor, and having a strong support system can help you navigate the ups and downs along the way.

In addition to setting clear goals and surrounding yourself with a supportive network, it is crucial to stay adaptable and open to change as you chart your course towards success. The path to success is rarely straightforward, and there will be obstacles and challenges along the way. By remaining flexible and willing to adapt to new circumstances, you can overcome these challenges and continue moving forward towards your goals. Remember, failure is not the end of the road but rather a stepping stone towards greater success. Embrace failure as an opportunity to learn and grow, and use it as motivation to keep pushing forward.

As you continue on your journey towards success, it is important to celebrate your victories, no matter how small they may seem. Acknowledge your hard work, dedication, and progress towards your goals, and take the time to recognize and appreciate your achievements. By celebrating your successes, you can boost your confidence and motivation, as well as remind yourself of how far you have come. Remember, success is a journey, not a destination, and it is important to savor the milestones along the way.

Ultimately, charting your course towards success requires perseverance, dedication, and a clear vision of what you want to achieve. By setting clear goals, surrounding yourself with a supportive network, staying adaptable to change, and celebrating your victories, you can continue on your path towards success with confidence and determination. Remember, success is not a destination but a journey, and by staying true to your goals and aspirations, you are taking important steps towards achieving your dreams. Stay focused, stay motivated, and keep charting your course towards success. Success is within reach – keep pushing forward.

- Final thoughts and words of inspiration

As we come to the end of our discussion, it is important to reflect on the key points that have been covered and leave you with some final thoughts and words of inspiration. Throughout this exploration, we have delved into various aspects of the topic and sought to provide a comprehensive understanding of the subject matter. From examining the historical context to exploring contemporary applications, we have endeavored to shed light on the complexities and nuances of the topic.

One of the key takeaways from this discussion is the importance of resilience and perseverance in the face of challenges. Life is full of ups and downs, and it is inevitable that we will encounter obstacles along the way. However, it is how we respond to these challenges that ultimately defines our character and shapes our path. By maintaining a positive attitude and staying focused on our goals, we can overcome even the most daunting of obstacles.

Another important point to remember is the power of passion and purpose. When we are driven by a deep sense of purpose and fueled by passion for our work, we are capable of achieving great things. It is this fire within us that propels us forward, even in the face of adversity. By nurturing our passions and staying true to our values, we can tap into a wellspring of motivation that will sustain us through the toughest of times.

In addition to resilience and passion, it is essential to cultivate a growth mindset. This means being open to new possibilities, embracing challenges as opportunities for growth, and constantly seeking to expand our knowledge and skills. By adopting a growth mindset, we can transform obstacles into stepping stones and turn setbacks into opportunities for learning and development.

As we navigate the complexities of life, it is also crucial to cultivate a sense of gratitude and appreciation for the blessings that surround us. By taking the time to acknowledge and celebrate our achievements, no matter how small, we can cultivate a sense of fulfillment and contentment that will sustain us through difficult times. Gratitude is a powerful force that can transform our perspective and imbue us with a sense of joy and abundance.

In summary, it is important to remember that we are not alone on this journey. Surround yourself with a supportive community of friends, family, and mentors who can provide guidance, encouragement, and perspective when you need it most. Lean on these relationships in times of struggle and lean into the wisdom and experience of those who have walked the path before you. By building a strong support network, you can weather the storms of life with grace and fortitude. You have within you the power to overcome challenges, pursue your passions, and achieve your goals. By cultivating resilience, passion, a growth mindset, gratitude, and a supportive community, you can navigate life's ups and downs with strength and grace. So go forth with confidence, knowing that you have the tools and the support you need to create a life of purpose, fulfillment, and joy.